Tragedy to Triumph!

Discover the secret to gaining victory over abuse.

written by Catherine
edited by Jann McCall

Distributed by
Texas Media Center
1-800-795-7171
www.texasmediacenter.com

Cover Design by Catherine & Sign Advantage

ISBN: 0-9715185-0-5

Printed in the United States of America
Color House Graphics, Inc., Grand Rapids, MI 49508

Contents

Introduction

You may have experienced tragedies in your life or you may know someone who has or is presently. This book is a recollection of events in the lifetime of Catherine that should have ended in certain tragedy, beginning with her infancy through her adult life, but instead lead to triumph.

Catherine has told her story on numerous occasions and used her past hardships to reach out and counsel many children and adults. She knows that there are thousands of others who need this hope and inspiration to carry on their lives and live in victory. No one should go through life living as a victim of circumstances, but instead use each circumstance as a learning tool and rise above the event. All facets of life are applicable to being a success! Too often, we hear the opposite. People have used their tragedies as an excuse to give up the race, to attract attention to themselves by other's pity, or as crutch to help them to accept being handicapped. We are accountable for every moment of our life, every talent and resource given us, every opportunity, and the example we live while others watch the steps we take.

The events told are all true. Some may be quite shocking and others as normal as your own life. The story is not told for the purpose of thrilling the mind with gore and horror but is told for the relevant information to demonstrate to the reader that the writer has the experience from which to speak out and encourage.

"Persons" key

Dad - The father who adopted Catherine from infancy along with "Mother".

Mother - The mother who adopted Catherine from infancy while married to her "Dad".

Mom - The stepmother who entered into Catherine's life at age 11 by marriage toher "Dad".

Bud - The brother who was adopted just days prior to Catherine's adoption and a part of her family the majority of her childhood.

Pauline - Catherine's biological mother who gave her up for adoption.

Cindy, Sue Anne and Dan - Pauline's children and Catherine's 1/2 biological siblings.

Stan and Bob - Mom's children and Catherine's stepbrothers.

Ray - Catherine's first husband

Randall, Joel and Rachel - Ray and Catherine's children.

Ben - Catherine's 2nd husband and True Love.

Benjamin and Ashley - Ben and Catherine's children.

Chapter 1: Background

Catherine was born on August 19, 1960 at Hillcrest Memorial Hospital in Waco, Texas to a young woman (15 years old) by the name of Pauline. Pauline found herself pregnant and unable to raise a child at this age and her parents mandated that she give up the child for adoption.

Pauline's mother sought means to accomplish an adoption and asked her friends and acquaintances for information about adoption procedures. She mentioned this need to her beautician who knew of a couple trying to adopt a child. The beautician immediately contacted this couple to inform them of an unwed mother seeking adoption for her child and this couple enlisted the services of a private attorney. All arrangements were made in anticipation of the birth of this child.

This couple had been on a waiting list at an adoption agency in another part of Texas and had been waiting quite some time. Even with the possibility of a private adoption, they were not going to remove their name from the waiting list, in the event that the private adoption might never transpire. It is never certain that the biological mother will actually finalize the adoption, that biological family members will not interfere, or that a child will reach full term and be healthy. Consequently, it was logical for this couple to retain their option with the agency.

The private attorney kept the couple informed throughout the unwed mother's pregnancy. Much to their surprise, just weeks prior to the due date, the adoption agency phoned with wonderful news that a baby boy was awaiting their adoption. They were in shock! Should they or shouldn't they? They reasoned that this baby boy was available now and ready to come home with them. There was no guarantee of the private adoption, so they quickly responded to the adoption agency and went to pick up their son. They were so very excited to have finally been given the opportunity to raise their own child.

Just a few weeks later, they received a call that the unwed mother from the private adoption was entering the hospital to give birth. They were told to remain close to the telephone for further word. Hours later, they received news that a baby girl was born and would be ready to go home with them in just a few days.

This couple was not prepared for two children at one time, but had always dreamed of having a boy and a girl and knew that this opportunity now existed. The only question was, could they handle raising two infants at once and were they financially able? The couple debated because the wife had always wanted a baby boy and the husband had always wanted a boy and a girl. Therefore he really wanted to follow through with the private adoption and she later agreed.

Quickly, they phoned the attorney and requested that he make all the legal arrangements for transfer of the child to them. Pauline was told that this couple was from another country and that she would never have to worry about this child again. She was instructed, that for her own peace of mind, that it would be best for her not to dwell on the birth of her baby. She was advised to simply view the situation as a short detour before getting on with the rest of her life. It all sounded great to her so she quickly, and without hesitation, signed the adoption agreement.

The new parents couldn't believe their eyes when they saw their beautiful infant girl. She had a dark complexion like a little Mexican baby, with jet black hair and dark brown eyes. She was perfect! A baby girl that any parent would be proud of! They were elated to be the parents of two cute little babies, a boy and a girl! It was as though they were twins. Everybody assumed that they were twins and the work involved in caring for them was the same. These two little babies were only thirty days apart in age.

The boy was named Bud. The name "Bud" had been added to the rest of his name so that he would not be called Jr. and that was the name that he would be called. The girl was named Catherine. The only reasoning behind this name was that is was a pretty name and besides, Catherine the Great was a famous name. They called her Cathy for short. At times they called her "Chatty Cathy" after they bought her a baby doll with that name and because she became quite a talkative little person.

Their first home was on 15th Street in Waco, Texas. This was convenient because it was directly across the street from the grandparents (parents of the father) and if they needed help, well, it was just a short few steps away. When you have two infants, the likelihood of needing help is sure.

The new mother of two was at first "overjoyed" with the additional tasks, but this joy quickly turned into "overwhelmed". To understand more about her ability to deal with these new stresses, an insight into her past is helpful.

She had been one of the youngest of nine children, five brothers (all older, except one) and three older sisters. She was raised mostly by her older sister Faye who loved her dearly and took her everywhere with her. She ran away to marry her first husband at the age of 15, against her father's wishes. They were married only a short time when she found out that she was pregnant. Toward the end of her pregnancy, she learned that her husband was under arrest for the gang raping of a young woman. He was found guilty and sent to prison, leaving her to raise their son alone while facing the humiliation of having been married to a man who was capable of this gross sin. She felt uneasy at home with her family and decided that she wanted to move to California. The family refused to allow her take the baby with her because she had no means of support for herself or the baby. Regardless of their advice, she left for California, leaving the baby with her older sister Esther. She felt the guilt of abandoning her son, the pressure of her husbands deeds, and the pain was unbearable. The stress was so tremendous that she buckled. She suffered a nervous break-down and admitted herself into a Mental Institution upon the advice of one of her brothers. She didn't stay there long when she decided to leave the institution with a 57 year-old married man who was a severe alcoholic. He told her that he had refused to obtain a legal divorce for religious reasons. She stayed with him for a few years before finally leaving. Soon after that, she began wandering from town-to-town and eventually state-to-state not knowing her own identity. She was apparently just running from reality to escape the pain. After the family had searched for her a few weeks, they determined to obtain legal custody of her child in the event that medical attention might be necessary or for anything else which would require their legal authority. A few months later, she was located in another state and returned to her family. The family sought treatment for her and she was eventually declared well. In the elapsed years, however, since abandoning her son, the child had bonded with her sister, Esther. The family thought it best to keep the child in Esther's custody since there was no certainty of her continued mental stability.

A few years later, Mother met Bill while waitressing at a little cafe and they eventually married. Bill had been previously married as well. He had gone into a law enforcement career with the Texas DPS and was assigned to the Weights and Measures enforcement. He was a good-looking officer and proud of his accomplishments but found that his paycheck of $300.00 a month was quite small for raising a family, so he changed his career to that of a truck driver. The pay was much better, but the hours were atrocious. He was gone for several days at a time and then home for a few, making it difficult for Mother with two small infants. On the brighter side, she would not have to work outside of the home now and could focus just on the care of her newly adopted babies.

There were many times when Dad would come home to find mother in a state of depression. He would try to help as much as possible, but she never really acted appreciative of his help or lifted out of the depression. He thought that this stage would pass soon, maybe when the babies were older and their care became easier.

An opportunity arose within the company to move to Dallas. Mother and Dad liked the idea of moving to fresh surroundings and the move was made. They rented a small place in Lake Dallas for a few months while looking for a home to buy which they found in Carrolton, Texas. The babies were now about 12 months old. They found a nice little three bedroom brick home with a fenced back yard on School Street. Just perfect for raising the babies. Mother quickly made friends with the neighbors who also had young children. The babies spent much time playing with their neighbor friends.

Chapter 2: First Childhood Memories

I can now remember a few details of my life at the age of two years old, however, the memories that I have are mostly gruesome. My brother Bud and I shared a bedroom with two baby beds. My bed displayed a pastel bear decal along with three spinning rattle balls at the foot of the bed to entertain me when I was bored and waiting for Mother to get us out of bed. Bud and I eventually learned how to crawl out of those baby beds and would take turns visiting in each other's bed. We played with our toys in our room together. I was told that Bud had learned to walk at the age of 8 months and that I learned shortly thereafter due to my competitiveness and desire for attention. Bud had only to smile to get Mother's notice, but I had to do much more if I ever hoped to receive Mother's recognition.

Mother didn't hold me and rock me like she did with Bud, but she was quick to explain that I was not an affectionate baby. She said that I rejected her because I didn't want to be held and, consequently she spent most all of her time with Bud. I'm certain that I was into everything and must have been a very curious baby. Maybe she thought that I didn't want attention, but I was just a busy baby and not a lap baby.

I had a strong will too. I remember sitting in my high chair crying because Mother wanted me to eat LIVER! Little Cathy does not eat Liver! Little Bud didn't either, but she didn't get angry with him, only angry with me. I realized at a very young age that I was not equal to Bud in her eyes. In fact, she really didn't even like me very much, she just tolerated me. My Daddy loved me though. He always spent time with Bud and me on the weekends after having been gone on his truck route. He later told me that he noticed how Mother shunned me, so he had tried to spend extra time with me. When Mother watched this extra attention given to me, it aroused her jealousy and she would demand that my Daddy play with Bud. Many arguments ensued regarding this as we grew. I can remember her telling him that I was not to sit in his lap. Sometimes he would tell me to run on just so that he wouldn't have to listen to her complain and other times he would put up with the nagging and let me sit there anyway. I always knew how much he loved me.

I was told that I was a very smart baby and toddler. A strong desire to please motivated me most of the time.

I was toilet-trained very easily at an early age and never had any difficulties with accidents EXCEPT one time. When I was three years old, the dreadful accident occurred that I will never forget. I was dressed in a pretty pink dress and accidentally pooped my panties at home. My mother began yelling and screaming at me and jerked me into her bathroom where my little potty chair stayed. She took off my panties and dumped the "mess" into the potty yelling that this is where the "shit" belongs. I was crying uncontrollably at the yelling when she turned and took my face down to the potty screaming, "See that mess. That's where it belongs; not in your panties." As I continued to cry as she forced my face into the potty chair, Mother's rage escalated. "You'll never do this to me again," she declared as she reached into the potty chair to retrieve some of its contents. Then with a fistful of poop, Mother made me EAT IT!!! I screamed in horror, but she was relentless. Thank goodness she didn't make me swallow it all because I was already beginning to vomit. I guess she thought that she would have a bigger mess, so she let me spit out the remainder, but the remnant was still caked to my tongue and teeth. She grabbed the bar of soap and scrubbed my tongue off and then I began to taste the soap. It was somewhat better but still sickening. I can't remember how it all ended except that Mother ordered me to my room for the remainder of the day which actually sounded good to me. I feel that I can really take offense to someone saying, "Eat _____ and die!" now that I have personally tasted this experience.

I remember many other screaming sessions and severe spankings while living in that house. Some of them were deserved, like the time that I got angry with Mother for going next door with Bud and without me. While staying alone, boredom crept in accompanied with mischievous ideas. It occurred to me that it would be great fun to poke a few holes in the white vinyl hassock with an ink pen that I had found. When Mother returned and discovered that, I received the worst beating ever.

Not all memories at that home were bad though. I do remember playing outside in my backyard with the neighbor girl named Angie and a few other kids. We had a swing set and a little swimming pool. I have a photo of Bud and me trading swimsuits once in our pool. Mother must have thought it was cute and snapped a picture.

It was while we lived in this home that all of my hair fell out. Mother and Dad took me to the doctor to learn the cause and even he was puzzled. The doctor reasoned that I might have ingested some type of poison or had a high untreated fever, which was quite likely since I was not allowed to cry when I was sick. My Dad asked for a remedy and was told that there was none and then my dad asked the doctor for permission to cut off all the remaining hair since it was falling out by the handful. My dad was crushed because I had such beautiful dark thick hair. After my hair was cut, it eventually grew back, but never as thick as before.

We had a black Lincoln with red interior. I can remember the pull down arm rest in the back seat that Bud usually occupied. I wanted to sit there, but he would cry to Mother to get his way.

Was I jealous? Absolutely!!!

Chapter 3: Troy

Soon, Daddy had another opportunity to make a change to build a home in the country. He and Mother had searched for quite some time to find affordable land in a nice area that he could raise a few cattle on, build a small pond, have a hay field and a big garden. He found just the right spot in a rural area of a small little town called Troy (which is only 7 miles from Temple, Texas. The little rural town that was closest was called Bell Falls but there was only a little gas station there and the population was 50 persons. Troy was the town where we went to church and school and Daddy went to the Barber and such. If Mother needed to buy groceries or clothes or take any of us to the Doctor, we went to Temple, just 7 miles south of Troy. Daddy was able to relocate his work to the Waco office. He worked for a large trucking company named Central Freight Lines. Central was a Texas Freight service which meant that he didn't have to drive out of state.

The land was approximately 54 acres and they had a beautiful white Austin stone house built right in the middle. The house was beautiful and huge. There were 4 bedrooms that were all very large, a den, dining, kitchen with separate eating area and two bathrooms and a two car garage. Our den was decorated in black Naulgahyde couch and chair with some dark wood coffee table and end tables. Hey! Don't laugh! Black naulgahyde was in style at that time. My bedroom was equipped with a light colored wooden double bed, double dresser and end tables that all matched. It was very pretty with a pastel pink bedspread and curtains to match in a contemporary fashion. Well, it was contemporary in 1964. Bud had a larger room with 2 twin beds and chest of drawers to match. The only room in the house that was carpeted was the master bedroom with that lovely avocado sculptured green carpet. Avocado green can get old in a very short time. I can't stand the color to this day.

The fourth bedroom was the Guest Room and that is eventually where my old upright piano sat. I didn't begin piano lessons until age 9 but since I was just learning to play, they thought that they could only bear the practice sessions if I was in the other end of the house right off the kitchen and utility area and just before the garage.

On the weekends when Daddy was home, we would all sit down to eat meals together in the kitchen eating area. Everyone had his place: Daddy sat at the head, Mother at his left hand, Bud at his right and me at the foot of the table. The table had chairs for 6 persons so there were chairs between me and the others. I liked sitting at the foot of the table because I could see right into my Daddy's eyes when he was home.

Daddy immediately built a small pond in front of the house, where I learned to swim at age 5. I hated my swimming lessons because I had a really mean and cruel teacher - my Mother! I remember when she had told me to extend my arms farther as she was holding my body to keep from sinking and when I cried, she dunked me and I tried again and she yelled at me again to extend my arms farther. Then she said that my swimming suit strap must be getting in my way and so the stripped me naked. I was so embarrassed that I began crying but she then informed me that I was going to go under the water again if I didn't shut up and so I held in the tears and sniffles and tried again. I believe that this was my final lesson because I was determined to never have to swim naked in front of my brother again and I didn't want to be dunked anymore so I worked very hard to get it right. I can even remember my red swimming suit that she stripped off. The original pond was probably only 50 yards in diameter, but it wasn't nearly large enough to keep from drying up or to even look good, so eventually, when we were 6 or 7 years old, he increased the size to about 2 1/2 acres. It was great! Daddy had someone come out and stock some fish in it, especially catfish. He also bought a little flat bottom fishing boat with twin engines. Bud and I both equipped with oars that is! There was a small little island to the left of the pond (if you are facing the main gravel roadway) and the cattails grew up all around the island. Bud and I would take the little boat there and make passages through the reeds and try to find our way precisely back through our trail that we had made. It was great fun exploring. We eventually called the island "Duck Island" because some wild ducks landed and took up residence there and then Daddy got a few big white ducks from a friend and they liked the island also. There was only one problem for the ducks there though, it was also a favorite spot for the snakes. It was common to see Water Moccasins swimming around and several other types. It seemed as though there choice diet was duck eggs. Every time our little lady duck would lay a few eggs, the snakes would eat them. This little lady duck had some peculiar eggs. They were soft-shelled. You could squeeze it or drop it and it wouldn't break, you literally had to cut a hole in it and tear it. We ate a few of the unfertilized eggs before the snakes found them.

We had a major project to do almost immediately after moving in and that was to put a barbed-wire fence around the property. My Daddy was so very strong. He dug some of those post holes with a manual post hole digger. I'm almost sure that he had an auger tool hooked up to his tractor too since I can remember riding from hole to hole on the red tractor. For a little 5 year old girl, building fences was great fun, especially when you are getting to spend time with your Daddy!

Great fun seemed to end almost as quickly as it had begun. Daddy's week long vacation spent building the fence was over before we realized and now back to the same old rut. Being bossed around by my brother Bud. It was bad enough to be bossed around but especially when you are a first born child and natural born leader. I didn't take well to being ordered by little baby that got his way all the time. If I refused to play what he told me to, then he'd run go tell Mother and I would get a spanking and screaming or even worse. If he was in the mood to play Cowboys and Indians and he wanted to be the cowboy, then guess who the Indian was. He got the nice tree house fort and I had to go climb some rugged tree, he got the nice Rifleman rifle set and I got an old stick for a rifle. He was very selfish. He had gotten this really nice Rifleman rifle and pistol set for his birthday and would not share even one little piece and Mother wasn't going to make him either. Since he wanted to play Cowboys and Indians all day out in the hot sun, I had to play or else. The "or else" was usually never worth trying out because it consisted of several licks with a belt (usually 7 - 10 and they didn't just land on my buttocks - anywhere on my backside from my neck to my ankles) or standing in the corner (usually for at least an hour but more likely 2 - 3 and there were times that I stood there for 7 - 8 hours and I'm not lying either)! If I had already stood there for 3 - 4 hours and I was asked when my time was up if I would then say I was sorry, I would indignantly say that I didn't do it and therefore I would get more time. The next time I was asked (3 or so hours later) I would just say I was sorry so I could get out. Your legs and feet can really ache after standing 7 - 8 hours at a time. It didn't matter if I was innocent or guilty at that point. She wasn't really interested in know-ing the truth anyway, she was just satisfied that I was out of her way for a while. One time, as I got older and wiser, I had been standing in the corner and hour and a half when I got a brainstorm idea. I had a tiny little wart on my left ring finger knuckle. If I could make it bleed, then maybe she would let me out early. So I was brave and bit it off and boy did it bleed. It worked! She was so busy trying to clean it up that she forgot to put me back in!!!

And, the wart was gone forever!!!

There were other times that she wouldn't feel sorry for me or take care of me though. I had this problem where I couldn't catch my breath when I would cry real hard. She swore that I was just a rotten child that was intentionally holding my breath to the point that I would pass out cause I had a bad temper, and if I did happen to pass out, then I would awaken to a serious beating for it. I would try really hard not to pass out, but it was impossible. One time, I think that I was about 5 years old, I was swinging on my swing set and she yelled at me about something and I began to cry and then next thing I knew, I was under the swing looking up from the ground at her yelling at me how stupid my temper was and how I was going to pay now. She beat my butt and put me in my room for the rest of the day. It happened at about noontime, so I had been banned to the room until the next day. I don't even remember if she fed me supper. I certainly wouldn't doubt it if she hadn't. There was another time that Bud and I had been bouncing on this bed and jumping around, when we were about 6 years old, and he pushed me and I fell off the bed onto the tile floor and it knocked the wind out of me and I tried to cry and ask for help but instead, I passed out. Again, I awake to see her screaming at me, saying that the passing out trick was only going to get me a spanking and that I was going to get extra licks for jumping on the bed. I tried to tell her that Bud pushed me off the bed and he denied it, so I was off for my beating. She turned and told Bud, "You know you're not suppose to jump on your beds" and he nodded in agreement and that was that. No punishment for her dear sweet little baby, who could do no wrong.

He was always thinking up some kind of trouble for us and he would talk me into joining in and actually carrying out his plan and I would always do it because I wanted him on my side. If he was mad at me, then he could get me into more trouble with Mother, and he knew it and used it to the full extent. This evening's plan was sure to be a lot of fun though. He brought in his little red kerosene lantern. It was little, but it was real. It really worked. He said that we could play like we were camping in his closet so we closed the closet door and he gave me the matches to light the lantern, so I did. Six year olds don't really think about adults having senses such as smell or hearing if they are a room away, but once the smell of burning kerosene and smoke passed the bedroom door, she came running to see what was on fire. To her surprise, her two little geniuses were at play with a lit lantern. When asked what we were doing, we said that we were playing camping and she asked who started the lantern and Bud said, "SHE DID!" He didn't bother to inform her that it was his brilliant idea or even say that he helped. I was jerked out of the closet by my ear and she yelled something about how I could have burned the whole house down if the clothes had of caught fire, and then I got my usual beating and sent to bed. Thanks a lot Bud! By the way, he got to go watch TV for a while before having to go to bed.

It is an understatement to say that she had no compassion for me, even if I was sick. I had a really bad cough once when I was six or seven and she came in my room and told me to be quiet. I told her that I couldn't stop coughing and she said that I was keeping her and Bud awake and that if I woke them again, she would send me out of the house. Well, I finally drifted off to sleep and accidentally coughed out loud, not muffling the noise into my pillow, and there she came. She jerked me up and took me into the garage and put me into the back seat of the car and told me that I wouldn't bother anyone out there and that I wasn't to come into the house until the next morning after everyone woke up. I laid there and cried myself to sleep. It was cold out there and I didn't have a blanket or a pillow and that old vinyl is cold until you lay real still and warm up a spot, but don't move at all, cause then you have to start all over warming up your spot again.

I was rarely sick, but I remember catching the flu one time when I was about 8 years old and I was so very sick. I woke up in the middle of the night and realized that I had to throw up so I got up and ran across the hall into the bathroom and it was pitch dark. I didn't have time to turn on the light so I just ran to where I knew the toilet was and there it came! Before I could even get my head down into the toilet. After the first wave hit, I was a better aim and was able to hit the inside of the toilet. I was crying and I guess I was too loud and woke up Mother. She turned on the bright bathroom light and started yelling at me about the mess I made and saying I was going to clean it up, not her because I knew better than to throw up on the wall and the tile floor. She wet a rag and threw it in my face and yelled, "Clean this up and it better be done right!" After I got through with the last wave of vomiting, I began to clean up all the mess. I don't know what I had eaten, by I remember bright red and orange chunks everywhere. It smelled so bad that I almost threw up again trying to clean it up, but somehow I managed. When it was all over, I returned to my bed and cried myself to sleep thinking about how cruel she was.

There was one time that she had to take care of me though. See, Granny (Mother's mother) had come to visit for the very first time at our new home and she was pretty old. She seemed like a very sweet lady though. She needed to take an afternoon nap so Mother decided to take Bud and me for a little walk around the pond. Bud said something ugly to me and I told him to shut up. She told me that I wasn't to talk to him that way and I rebutted that he had talked mean to me and then she yelled at me to quit arguing with her and she looked down on the ground and conveniently found a wood wedge (left from the roof corner as they had built our house) and whacked me over the back of the head with it. Well, she surprised herself that time because she gashed my head open and there was blood everywhere. She had to think quickly cause she didn't want her mother to know what she had done. She ordered me, in a very hushed demanding tone, to not make a single tear fall or even a whimper when we went inside the house and straight to the bathroom. I did as I was told and we made it past Granny without her even noticing the blood all down the back of my dress. She took me into the bathroom and washed the blood out of my hair and got the bleeding to stop and sent me to my room to get clean clothes on, meanwhile she cleaned the blood out of my dress. Yes, she actually cleaned it herself. I found clean clothes and put them on and went outside to my little dog. I had a little toy terrier that was black and white and if I ever needed someone to talk to or cry to, he would always enjoy listening. I really wanted to tell Granny, but I knew that she would only be with us for a few more days, and that when she was gone, I would pay dearly, besides Mother would come up with some lie of an excuse to explain the gash on my head. Oh well, it was a thought, but only a thought. My little dog would just have to do.

No one ever knew about her gashing my head open until I was a teenager and had gone to a beauty shop to get a hair cut. The beautician asked me how I got that scar on my head. She said that it was an inch long. Well, it was OK to tell her, because by then, I wasn't living with my mother anymore.

Living on a farm in Troy had its good points and bad points. The good points from a child's perspective are very few. There was lots of space to play. We weren't restricted to play just in our yard. We could play anywhere on our 54 acres, the woods, the creek, the gullies, the pond and sometimes even the neighbor's land. Our neighbor's didn't use their old barn anymore and so sometimes Bud and I would slip off to explore. It was really cool! We could play all sorts of things, like pretending we were farmers, or Bonnie and

Clyde hiding out while on our getaway from the last bank robbery. We had great imaginations. He always made me have to be the one to get shot or killed. He was always the winner. I wanted to play house up at the old barn but he refused to play my silly girl games. I actually learned to be quite good at boy stuff and eventually Mother started calling me a "Tomboy". Well it seems to me that if she wanted me to act like a little girl or a little lady, then she would allow me to play the games that I wanted to play, but that was never even considered. Bud voluntarily agreed to play 1 game that I wanted to play when we were about 8 years old and it lasted a whole 20 minutes and that was to play, "Store". I was the clerk for a while and he was the customer with lots of play money, then we would switch, but he didn't let me have as much money as he had used, he insisted that I was a poor old granny. Oh well, at least we were in MY room playing MY game.

The bad points about living in the country was that there were no friends around. Our closest neighbors were some old farmers that lived about a 1/4 mile up the road to the east. They had no kids though, they were old. There was a family that lived further up their road another 1/4 mile and they had a farm too, but their kids were too little. Our family went up to visit their family a couple of times over the 7 years that we lived there but we weren't close. Another 1/2 mile down the main road to the east lived the Krause's. They were old people too. The only people around that weren't old was Candy's family. She lived 1/4 - 1/2 mile south of the Krause's. I really liked Candy and her family. They were very nice. Candy was a Senior at my school and a Baton Twirler. She was really good and really beautiful. She had long straight brown hair and very pretty eyes and a sweet smile. I always wanted to grow up and be like her. My brother thought she was pretty too. He would sit and stare and her when we would visit and tell me later how pretty she was.

A few times we would go Trick-or-Treating. We drove to each of the neighbor's houses, but when everyone lives so far apart, it takes forever and you don't seem to get as much candy but on the other hand, the ladies made some extra special treats for us and we would go in and visit for a while at each home, and while we were there we would eat a popcorn ball or special cookies and milk. All of the people knew us and would comment on how cute we were and how much we had grown. Trick-or-Treating in those days was safe in our little safe rural town. We only heard of something really bad happening in some other large town in Texas when I was 10. Some man had put a razor blade in an apple and a child found it and the news media was alerting all parents to be careful and check the child's candy. So each year Mother and Daddy would go through our sacks to check for unsafe items and also pick some of their favorites out. When we were this age, we never knew what Trick or Treating meant and the significance of Satan's High Day, so you could say that we were ingnorant in this area.

By age 5, Mother had taught me how to wash the dishes and clean the table. I was actually excited to learn this until I found out that this would be my job from now on. Every single night, I had to wash all the dishes, even the pots and pans and I mean that this was without any help! Daddy had installed a dishwasher, but that was only for the dishes after I washed all the food off of them. It didn't really save any time except for drying them. Mother always put them away the next day. I did them every night regardless of how I felt or if something special was going on or a special show on the television. She taught me how to push a chair up to the sink and hop up there and wash everything, even the messiest of pans. Even if was sick, I still had to do the dishes. One evening, I felt so bad that I asked if I could just go to bed. Her comment was that I wasn't about to try to get out of doing my job by claiming that I was sick. I promised her that I wasn't faking it and Daddy even looked at me and said that he could tell that I didn't look well. Everything in the room was glassy looking. He felt my forehead and said that I had a fever. She was then mad that he was taking up for me and told me to get my dinner eaten so I could get my dishes done and then I could go to bed. Daddy spoke up and told me that if I wanted to go to bed, then go on and he would do the dishes for me. I was relieved! My Daddy was so sweet. I really was sick and I went straight to bed! She and he continued to argue after I left the room. He even commented about how cruel hearted that she could be sometimes.

There were times that I wasn't perfect at this job. One evening, I accidentally left some food in the sink strainer. There were a few green beans and soap bubbles there when Mother went into the kitchen for something. She called out in her usual voice as I quickly recognized that I was in trouble for something. She called me over to the sink and pointed at the food scraps that had not been emptied. She yelled out at me as she shoved my head down into the sink (killing my chest and ribs as the counter top edge was only chest high for me) asking, "What is that mess doing there?!!! and I told her that I forgot to dump out the strainer and that I was ... I didn't get to finish my sentence before I had been whacked over the head and shoulders with the iron skillet. I screamed out in pain and she pulled my head back by my hair and told me that forgetfulness was no excuse. I never forgot it again!

Another big "no-no" was to put left-over food away improperly. One afternoon, Mother had gone into the kitchen and opened the refrigerator door to find the leftover meatloaf from the night before. She loved cold meatloaf sandwiches! I had taken the meatloaf out of the pan, that she had cooked in the night before, and placed it on a sheet of Saran Wrap and wrapped it tightly and neatly so that no air could get in. I knew that it would be yucky if air got to it and I thought that I did a good job. Well, she grabbed me by the neck and hair and had the meatloaf in her other hand and had it up in face screaming, " What is this crap! Why did you mess up my meatloaf?" I explained to her that I thought I did it right and she took me by the throat and pinned me up against the wall and slapped me back and forth across my face three times, full open handed slaps and back handed slaps, causing cuts inside of my mouth. And then she yelled something else at me before she screamed at me to get out of her face as she threw me down to tile floor. I landed in a prime position to then be kicked right in my buttocks to somersault over and land a few feet from her. I ran away from her screaming uncontrollably and sobbing viciously! I was awe struck! This was the beginning of a slight bit of bitter hatred towards her.

We went to school at Troy Elementary School, but it was physically located at the same site as the Junior High and High School building and we all shared the same gymnasium. My first teacher was Mrs. Rogers, and Bud had the other 1st grade teacher who was much younger. Mrs. Rogers seemed, to me, to be about ready to retire since she was so old, but she was a good teacher. She scared me a few times and I minded her extremely well except for the time that Bud had gotten into trouble and I heard him crying in the hall. I went out to see if he was OK and Mrs. Rogers found me out of the class and ordered me back into her classroom and I started screaming and crying that I wanted to stay with my brother. I was scared that his teacher would hurt him or something. Mrs. Rogers demanded that I return to my seat after my fit was calmed down and I did as I was told. I just couldn't understand why she wouldn't let me stay with him.

I was very motherly to Bud when we were at school. I would always take up for him. He was smaller than most of the other kids and he got picked on quite a bit. He also had a burr haircut and the kids would tease him and call him a "Bald-headed chicken-pluckcr". Well, no one was going to hurt my brother or tease him! I always kept my eyes and ears open while on the playground together, just to make sure everything was OK. We always rode the bus to school. We rode with all the kids from all grades. There were some nice high-school girls that would treat me special sometimes and let me sit by them or maybe I just pushed my way in sometimes and they tolerated me. They seemed nice though. One time I had wrecked on my bicycle on our little gravel rode by the spillway and scratched my face all up. Mother had put Methyolate on it and my whole right side of my face was colored red with scabby scratches and the older girls on the bus said that I looked like a cute little Indian girl to make me feel better. I was quite embarrassed to step foot on the bus.

Bud and I were never in the same class together at Troy. There were always two classes per grade level and they would place up apart. I'm sure that this was the best choice because I learned how to socialize apart from his criticism. He would always call me names in front of his friends and mine, thinking that he would look cool, but if he needed me for something, like getting a girl to like him, then he would lay off the name calling for a while. I guess most brothers are that way though.

His first girlfriend was Sherry and they were in the third grade. I was shocked when he told me that he kissed her by the water fountain. He was so shy that I thought he would never have the guts, but I was wrong. He had me invite her over to the house to spend the night with me so that they could be together and Mother thought that it was SO cute that he had a girlfriend, that she performed a little pretend wedding ceremony for them and he kissed his bride! Can you believe it? She would have killed me for this but for Bud, she thought it was cute and he kissed her right in front of Mother! I should have known that he liked her so much because one day, when Mother was invited to Sherry's mother's house for a Tupperware party or something, we kids were in Sherry's bedroom playing "Spin-the-bottle" and Bud definitely wanted to stay and watch. Bad thing was that we got caught in the middle of the game and I being the most unlucky spinner was the least dressed when caught. I was so embarrassed! I had just enough time to get mostly redressed before my mother came in to see, and the other mother didn't tell the details, so I lucked out a little.

My first boyfriend was Marty Cook. He was so very cute and he wasn't a scrawny little guy either. I felt that I had the best catch of all. Well, Bud owed me a big favor so I reminded him of that favor when I wanted Marty to spend the night. We were also in the third grade, but it was later during the school year. I certainly didn't feel that I could ask Mother to do the same little ceremony for Marty and me so Bud became a preacher instantly. It was very brief but it didn't really matter as long as he didn't forget the line - "You may now kiss the bride". Boy did he! I was shocked! He French Kissed me! I didn't even know what it was at the moment, but Bud told me later when I asked him why he stuck his tongue down my throat. OK, slightly exaggerated but only slightly. It was a French Kiss and I never forgot it. It was quite yucky for an 8 year old girl who was very naive. But I did have something to brag about to all the girls. I was married to the best looking guy at school and kissed by him!!!

My best girl friend was Melissa Wiley. She was a very pretty girl with long, blonde hair and light freckles and blue eyes. She talked kind of country sounding, but that was just her. We did everything together at school. She was smart and we had a lot in common except that she was a "lefty". I always thought it was so funny! Bud was a lefty too, but I used to think that only dummies were lefties since he didn't do very well in school. Mother let her spend the night with me a few times and we would stay up late playing with my Barbie dolls and making them new clothes. Mother had lots of scrap materials that we could cut out and sew up with needle and thread. I was actually getting to play girl games! She was even good at playing "Army" and "Cowboys and Indians" and it was much more fun having her on my side because Bud couldn't always make up new rules as we went along to make sure that he would win! This time, we would win!

As summer came, I was allowed to have a birthday party. I never remembered having a birthday party before, but I know that I had, because Mother showed us pictures of our 1st birthday party. We were only 30 days apart in age, so she would generally celebrate our birthdays together. This time, I would have my very own birthday party though. I got to invite several friends and we had it outside in the backyard. We played several games and had cake and stuff and my friends brought me some presents. I remember the present that my Daddy got for me most. He had previously taken me to pick it out at a very nice jewelry store. It was a Cinderella watch! Cinderella was wearing a pretty light blue ball gown and the watch band matched in light blue. I was so very proud of it. This was my most favorite gift of all!

My birthday party was sometime around August 19th and this meant that school was about to begin.

Fourth grade also had its landmark. That was the first year that I ever got sent to the Principal's Office. My teacher had sent everyone outside to play for recess. I left something in the class, so I got permission to run back and get it. When I walked into the room, I noticed the overhead projector still set up and I had always wondered how one worked. I looked at it closely and had seen the teacher turn it on several times so I plugged it in and turned it on and as I was curiously looking it over, when, in walked my teacher! She was mad! I was terrified! She told me that I knew better than to play with school equipment and I could have broken it and then she sent me to the office where I was certain that I would get the paddle. Well, the principal wasn't in her office and it took a little while for the teacher to find her so that she could tend to me. I certainly didn't explore anything while I waited. I sat nervously awaiting the paddle. When she got there, she talked to me sternly and I begged her not to spank me and she agreed not to this time, but if I ever snooped again, then I could count on it.

This was pretty terrifying for me because I usually never got into trouble except for talking and I was often in trouble for that. I talked so much in the second semester of 1st grade that I got a "C-" in citizenship on my 4th, 6 weeks report card. I knew that I couldn't take a "C" home, so I erased it carefully, found a red ink pen to match and changed it to an "A-". Mother never noticed, but the teacher did. When I took it back to turn it in I had forgotten to change it back to a "C-". My Mother spanked me severely for this. When my Daddy came home and found out that I had a "C-" in citizenship, and also tried to lie about it, then he also gave me a spanking. Oh I wished that I had just taken the report card home without making any changes, 'cause then I would have only gotten one spanking. That night, when I went to sleep, I had a nightmare about Mother spanking me with a belt all night long. When I would wake up and realize it was just a dream, I would fall asleep and dream it some more. I was so glad for morning to come.

It wasn't illogical to have a dream like that. There was a time that I had upset Mother and she called me into the living room to spank me. She held my left arm with one hand and the belt in the other and began to lash my behind as hard as she could swing the belt. Every time that she would lash, I would take a step forward and the steps got faster and faster as the lashings came faster and more furious and then suddenly, I tripped and fell to the ground on my face. She was more angry that I was so clumsy and so she gave me a few more while I was on the ground and these lashes landed wherever they chose. I got up after she finished, and was crying uncontrollably when she noticed that my tooth was broken. She asked my how this had happened and I told her that I tripped and fell and hit my tooth on the tile floor and she was then so upset with me, that she hit me a few more times as she screamed out what a clumsy ox I was and she ordered me outside into the backyard, yelling how she never wanted to see my face again. I sat on the swing seat and waited for her to calm down and let me in. Meanwhile, I still was unable to stop crying, but I had to cry with my lips shut because the cool Autumn air was hitting the exposed nerve of my tooth, causing excruciating pain! When I finally got to come inside the house, I ran into my bedroom to see the damages. It was so ugly. It broke off diagonal right across the middle of my front tooth.

Mother had been inside on the phone, calling the Dentist Office to set an appointment to repair the tooth for the next day. I was so glad that she didn't wait longer because I was in so much pain! I couldn't eat or drink. I don't know what she told the Dentist about how it happened, but I'm sure that it wasn't the whole truth. The dentist was able to make some kind of bonding cap on the tooth so that it was not apparent, unless you looked very closely. I was very happy that none of my friends had to see that!

Fourth grade was also the year that I began piano lessons. I was 9 years old and Mother insisted that I learn to play. My piano teacher's name was Candice. I was so eager to please her that I tried really hard. There was one drawback, Mother put my piano in the guest room which was in the other end of the house. Everything was fine until Winter and she did not heat that room unless a guest was coming. That makes sense, but at least open the door while I practice so my fingers wouldn't get so cold! I began crying one day because I really didn't feel like practicing right then and she came in there and told me that I wasn't going to come out until I practiced for 30 more minutes. I didn't play right and she came in there, jerked me up off my piano bench and held me up off the floor by my ears and screamed to me that I would practice right because she wasn't wasting her time and money to take me to my lessons. I promised that I would practice and said that I was sorry, as I screamed in pain. Finally she let me down and walked out of the room. Oh my ears hurt so bad, but there was no time to feel sorry for me now, or else I'd get more. I played as I was told. I didn't really gain anything from that practice session except for another lesson in human cruelty. I really hated her doing that stuff to me. I really wanted her to love me though. I mean, I loved her, why couldn't she love me? I wasn't ugly or deformed, but I was bad though. I was always bad. Maybe if I acted better, then she would love me.

I got pretty good at playing the piano. I even got good enough that she sat in the guest room and listened and even complimented me. I told her that there was a talent show coming up at school and that I would like to play. She said that she would talk to Candice and see what she could help me to prepare to perform. I was so excited! This would be my debut! When I went to my next lesson, Candice showed me the song that she wanted me to play for the talent show but it was a rinky-dink, baby-sounding song. I wanted to play "Fur Eloise". I asked her if I could play that song instead and I even played it for her, but she insisted that I wasn't ready to play that one. Well, I told Mother what she said and she agreed with ME!!! She liked "Fur Eloise" better also and told me to play it instead of Candice's choice.

The big night came and Mother fixed me up in my very best and even curled my hair. She always loved to hear people say how cute I was but got angry if they didn't also mention Bud. Anyway, the time came and they announced my name as my turn came up and I went forward and sat down, and noticed the gym at school was full of people. It was incredible! I wasn't a bit scared because I was going to do something that my Mother was excited about. I got up there and played "Fur Eloise" almost as well as Beethoven himself. When I finished, everyone applauded and I was so proud! I even saw Mother clapping! Candice was furious that I hadn't done as I was told, but I told her that my Mother told me that I could make the change, and she hushed. It felt so good to say that MY MOTHER said that I could. I felt that I had her approval. Everybody came up to her after the talent show and commented about how well I had played, and she was beaming!

Her approval was short lived though. Only a few months later, I saw her sitting and rocking Bud on the white hassock (you remember, the one I poked the holes in when I was 3 years old - yeah, that one). She was rocking him back and forth singing "Baby Bye - Baby Bye". It was not a real song, just one that she used to sing to him all the time when she would hold him in her lap and play with him or rock him. I passed through the living room, as she was there with him singing this, and I just decided to stop and ask, "Why don't you love ME like that?" She replied, " I don't know, I just don't." Then she began rocking and singing to Bud again and I went into my room and shut the door and cried into my pillow for a long time. I always knew that she didn't love me but I never thought that she would tell me so. I was hoping for her to say, "Of course I love you" and take ME into her lap and sing something to me, but that was just a dream.

Her words bounced around in my head daily. I wondered if there was anything that I could do to change her opinion or if this was just one of those matters that I would have to accept. I sat outside the house on the side lawn daydreaming of what it would be like to have my own baby girl. I would love her dearly and never harm her. I could give her all the attention that I had wanted. AND she would love me! Being her mother, she would automatically love me. I began daydreaming this dream on a regular basis. All I wanted to do was to grow up and get married and have a baby girl. Oh how nice that would be!

Well, summertime came and it sounded like it would be promising because I was going to spend some time at my Granny Letha's house. She lived somewhere in the Smithfield area in Ft. Worth. Daddy and Mother decided that they needed a vacation, just the two of them. Granny Letha seemed glad to have Bud and me visit, as long as we didn't argue and fight. I enjoyed going to her house because she had some pretty, white, Alaskan Spitz dogs and they had recently had puppies. She also had a bid garden to play or work in and she even cut my hair for me. All I had to do was ask and she said OK. She had some neat nifty hair cutting tool but it sure did pull as she cut it. After several days there, my Uncle D (not his true name) came by to visit. He was my very favorite uncle. He always paid special attention to me when he would visit us and this time was no exception. He offered to Granny Letha to take me for the weekend to give her a little break and she was glad to accept the offer.

I was thrilled! Just me and Uncle D. I tried to talk him into stopping for ice cream and all sorts of things but he had a Chiropractic appointment first and then we would go to his house. I sat patiently and waited for him to be finished and we were off again to his house. He talked to me for a few moments in the truck, as we headed to his house, to ask if I knew about the birds and the bees. I was totally unaware of what he was talking about and so he asked another question, "Do you know where babies come from?"

Well, when we got to his house, which was a lovely 2-story house on Mimosa street in the Dallas area (I can remember the street name because I always liked Mimosa Trees), he asked me if I would like to see where babies come from. Of course any 9 year old little girl wants to know where babies come from so I was quite attentive. He sat down on his living room sofa and asked me to come and see his drawing. He was sketching a picture of the male reproductive organ and the female reproductive organs. It was all so very interesting and informative but I was a little bit embarrassed to see the male part. I had only accidentally seen my daddy naked once as he had gotten out of the shower and forgot to lock the bathroom door and OOPS, I walked in on him and then quickly ran out, just totally embarrassed. We were a very private family and very modest so this picture was funny looking to me.

After explaining everything on paper, he asked me if he could take some pictures of me. I thought he meant real pictures. Well, he did, but he meant that I would be naked. I was embarrassed that he'd asked me but he assured me that no one else would ever see them, they would just be his special pictures of his special niece. He went to find a Polaroid Instant Camera to take pictures but I told him when he returned that I really didn't want him to do that so he said, "OK". He asked me to wait in the living room and he went into his bedroom and later called me in. I went in to see what he wanted and was surprised to see him lying in his bed under the covers. He asked me to shut the door as I had entered and then he asked me to undress. I was wearing a little orange shorts set and I was nervous. He told me that he just wanted to look and that he wouldn't hurt me.

I stood there by his closet door and my mind was racing trying to figure out what to do. I prayed a quick prayer asking Jesus to forgive me for my curiosity knowing that I should have never been interested in what he was showing me. I felt that it was all my fault for being in this spot because I had been too curious. Had I just refused to look at his drawings and asked no questions, then all of this would not be happening.

He spoke up again and said that he just wanted to see my pretty body and that there was nothing wrong with being naked. I knew that there was no way out so I did as he had told. I stripped down to my nudity. He told me to come over to the other side of the king size bed where he was lying and asked me if I wanted to see something and then he jerked back the covers and he was stark naked too! He exposed his whole self to me and asked me to do some "deeds" for him and he proceeded to sexually molest me for his own sexual gratification. I had NEVER been exposed to this type of activity and was very uncomfortable with all of his actions but I didn't know how to get out of it. He had already made me feel bad that I couldn't do enough for him because I was just too young and some things were too painful for my small body. I was very embarrassed about everything that he was showing me and making me do to him and certainly carried a lot of guilt because of this. Had I only not been so curious. It had to be my own fault.

His little lesson in "where babies come from" was just being taught on a "hands on" basis. After this, he asked me to take a bath and he would wash me. He went into the bathroom and drew the water and made it warm and began to gently wash me and tried to touch my private parts inside again but I kept pushing his hand away. Finally, the bath was over and I was allowed to get dressed but as I was dressing he told me how important it was that I never tell anyone what he had taught me because someone might not understand how special of a relationship we had and that he might go to jail. He asked me if I wanted him to have to go to jail and of course I wouldn't want that. He was my favorite uncle even if I didn't like what he had done.

The next day, I was still at his house and his family had all left for a while leaving us alone. Uncle D approached me to ask me if I wanted to come and learn and play some more in his room and I ran up the stairs to the bed where I was staying in. He kept begging me and I kept saying no. He came up to me as I was lying on the bed and rubbed my legs and shoulders trying to talk me into it and I told him that I never wanted to do that again and to please leave me alone. He got angry and walked out saying how I must not be his special girl anymore, but I really didn't care. I never wanted any of this to happen in the first place and I didn't care if he ever loved me again.

A day or so later, Mother and Daddy had come to pick us up. When they got there, Granny Letha told me to go into the other room to watch TV with Bud and she and Mother and Daddy stayed in the kitchen with the door closed. I tried to watch TV but was very curious about what they were talking about. I heard my name come up a few times and Uncle D's and Uncle P's but I couldn't really understand what they were talking about.

After 30 minutes or so, Mother and Daddy came out and told Bud and I that it was time to go. We gave Granny Letha a big hug good-bye and we were off.

It seemed like a very long drive and I was just getting tired when Daddy asked me a few strange questions about Uncle D. He asked me if any of his family were there when we went to his house or were we alone. He asked where all we went and what we did. Then he told me that Granny Letha had just told them about some big lie that I told to Uncle P about Uncle D. I was scared breathless!!! This was it, I would probably never be loved by my Daddy again and they would probably get rid of me for this one. He asked me straight out - Did you tell your Uncle P a big lie about you and Uncle D? I told him that I had not told any lie to anyone. He asked me another direct question. Did Uncle D undress in front of you or do anything else? I wouldn't answer and he then told me that I wasn't in any trouble at all as long as I was telling the truth. He assured me that I hadn't done anything wrong but to please tell him the truth. I was embarrassed to explain this in front of Mother and Bud but he insisted that I tell him right then. I told him that he had gotten naked and made me get naked too and that he was being nasty with me. Daddy then told Mother, "I'm sure that she's telling the truth, I wouldn't put anything past him. I've felt that he was sleeping with his own daughter for a while and I've seen how he looked at Linda when she was a teenager (that's Daddy's only real daughter that rarely comes to visit) and I would have never allowed Cathy to go anywhere with him. He and Mother continued to talk about it and Mother would occasionally make a statement about me not being truthful, but Daddy was adamant to believe me and then they both came to an agreement to believe me and to follow through with this matter.

I didn't know exactly what they meant but I was so happy that they actually believed me and gave me hugs and told me how sorry they were that I had to be with him. Yes! Even Mother!!! Daddy asked me one more question that would help him to prove that I was telling the truth. He asked me if I had seen anything on Uncle D that looked different. I wasn't sure what he was asking and he asked me if I had seen a scar on him. I told him that I saw one on his right side about in the middle of the right side under his pants. He got out a piece of paper and drew a section of a body, from the waist to the thigh area, and asked me to mark the spot where the scar was, and I did. Daddy was convinced! Then he asked me how it looked and I showed him about an inch and a half long. He said that I was right. Uncle D had previously had a surgery for a hernia and that was where his scare was and unless I had seen him naked, I wouldn't have known it was there. My Daddy is so clever!

The next weekend was terrible! We went to Granddaddy B's and Granny E's house and there was Aunt Nana and Uncle G. They told Bud and I to sit and watch TV in the Living Room and they went into the Kitchen and closed the door. I heard some of what they were saying. My Daddy started off telling them about the incidents that happened with the Uncles. I heard Aunt Nana say that she felt that I was lying and trying to cause trouble to get attention for myself and then Granny E spoke up and said that she didn't believe it either because I was telling something about both Uncles. Daddy brought up a logical explanation as to why Uncle P would mention this to Letha if it were true what Uncle D had done, to cover up for himself and just let her know that I was spreading WILD STORIES. That way, if any WILD STORIES came up about him then no one would believe me because I was just telling tales about all of my uncles. He had a wonderful plan to discredit me and cover for himself. He also explained to them that I wouldn't have known about his scar had I not seen him naked, but they didn't want to believe that either. They were then yelling at Daddy, telling him that they couldn't believe that he would believe his dirty, lying, tramp, little daughter and then to cause all of this trouble in their family, and Daddy told them as he left out, "Well I believe her and you can just close your eyes and not believe it if you want, but I'm going through with an attorney." He and Mother left out angrily and told Bud and me to come along. We drove home and they discussed it all the way home.

Daddy asked me if I would go take a lie detector test to prove to the family that this had really happened and I was more than OK with that. I wanted to be believed more than he wanted them to believe me. He had set an appointment with a man that does those kind of tests and Daddy took me to see him. First, they spoke a little while and then they came out and told me that it was my turn. Daddy didn't stay though. The man explained to me that it was really best that I do this like a big girl by myself and that way I would be able to tell him the whole truth. He first explained all of his equipment to me and promised that it wouldn't hurt a bit and then he asked me all sorts of questions like - my age, my address and whether or not I knew the difference between the truth and a lie. Then he asked me to explain everything that had happened. I told him the basics and he asked a few additional questions and then he hooked me up! I was shaking. I was worried that the machine would think I was not being truthful and that it was shock me dead! The man reassured me that it wouldn't hurt a bit and the questions began. At first I was very apprehensive, but after the general questions, I eased up some and found that this was very simple. When we were finished, the man told me that I had done a great job and that I could go get my Daddy and to please wait out in the office for Daddy. After another 10 minutes or so, Daddy came out and told me that he was very proud of me doing such a good job. He wanted me to know that he had already believed me before taking the test but now he could prove to others that I was telling the truth.

It seemed as though only a few weeks had passed when we were on our way to court. Daddy explained to me that he was trying to get his brother some psychiatric help so that he would never do anything like this again and he just wanted me to tell the people what had happened with Uncle D. I was pretty scared and I really wasn't sure what "Court" meant or looked like. We had to sit outside of the courtroom and couldn't hear any of the other things going on and Daddy was upset that he wasn't allowed inside. We waited for a long time and then a man came and talked to Daddy and Daddy looked at me and told me that it was time to go in and tell them what happened. I wanted Daddy to go with me but he explained that the judge said that he couldn't go and I would have to be a big girl and go tell the truth.

I walked into a very large room with wooden church pews on both sides facing the big chair up front where a man was sitting, who I was told was the judge. I was asked to sit in the chair just below the judge. He nodded hello and I was then introduced to the jury. This man told me that they were there to hear what I had to say but that they only wanted to hear the truth. Then someone approached me with a Bible and asked me if I would swear to tell the truth, the whole truth and nothing but the truth, so help me God, and I agreed. First off, were a few general questions that weren't real important and then he asked me specific questions about the incident.

Before we had gone into the courtroom, Mother had explained to me that I would need to use the proper words when I would tell other people in court what had happened and so she taught me the clinical terms for a female private was a "vagina" and the proper word for the male private is a "penis". I laughed at these unusual sounding names and she made me say them a few times and verify that I understood which sex they belonged to and told me that I wasn't to say "privates or tee-tee or weenie or ding-dong" to the people in the court. I understood that this was a big deal and I couldn't act like a little baby when I went in to tell what happened.

Well, during court questioning, I was asked to describe what had happened in Uncle D's bedroom. I told the least details as possible but I remembered to use the words that Mother taught me - "vagina and penis". Every time I had to say them and then explain to those people that I knew what they were, I would giggle. I was so embarrassed to say them or even talk about this stuff to all these people that I would occasionally giggle. The man asked me if I was telling the truth and I told him that I was. He then asked me if the man that I was telling about was in the courtroom there and if so could I point him out? Well that was easy, Uncle D was sitting to my right in a gray suit and I pointed him out, as asked. I felt sorry for him but I was sure that I was doing the right thing because I didn't want him to do this to any other girl.

Well, after I testified, I had to leave the courtroom again and sit out with Mother and Daddy. I told them that I told everything and they said that they were proud of me. A while later, the man came out again and this time all the other people came out too. The man told Daddy that they had lost the case. He told them that he felt that the jury didn't believe me because I was laughing. Daddy asked me why I was laughing and I told him that I was embarrassed to say those words. He didn't know that Mother had told me to say them and he told me that I just lost the case since I didn't take it serious enough to keep from laughing. Daddy just didn't understand that I giggled to keep from crying from embarrassment. Little girls don't say words like that, especially to a room full of adults!

By this time, I was sick of this whole thing. We had to walk out of the courthouse and they (the other family members) were all out there and they told Daddy that they couldn't believe that he put his own brother through all of that, and that this proved that I had been lying. Daddy still defended me and they then told him that he, nor I, were welcomed to any further family functions since we were going to continue to believe this.

I was shocked!!! It was as though my Daddy was being punished for something that his brother had done. Daddy wasn't trying to hurt his brother, but he wanted him to get some help before he did this to anyone else and now he was being shunned! Daddy was crushed! I could tell that this wounded him deeply, but I was happy that he stood by me and he knew that he had done the right thing.

I learned at a very young age that life isn't fair!

Our family became a little bit closer because of all of this. There was no other family support left. We tried to get our lives back to normal.

Our closeness didn't last long. Mother and Daddy began their arguing again and Mother was right back to her normal actions toward me. There were times that Daddy would call home for her to bring him home to spend the weekend with his family, and she would tell him that she wasn't in the mood to pick him up. He got angry and told her that she had better pick him up or he wouldn't leave her the car next time. Well, she got her shoes on and picked him up, but she wasn't happy to see him. But Bud and I were ecstatic! We waited for days to get to see him for the weekend. Besides, he was the one who always took us to church and church was awfully important to me. I was even being baptized soon. It took some talking to the preacher because he thought that I was too young to be baptized, but I assured him that I knew what I was doing and that it was essential that I do it then. The pastor finally agreed to baptize me and I knew that this was the most important decision of my entire life and future! Boy, that water surely was cold though!

When Daddy was home, we would always do something fun like work in the big garden, brand cattle, build a barn, go frog gigging in the lake, work on the car or the tractor - just all kinds of things. Daddy was lots of fun! He would teach us how to drive the car or the old pickup and also the red tractor. It was so funny when Daddy taught me to drive the tractor. He was on the trailer (being pulled by the tractor), loading on the bails of hay in the pasture. He yelled, "GO!" and so I let out on the clutch and pushed on the gas pedal and WHAM! Daddy fell off the trailer onto the ground. He yelled out at me, " I said not to pop the clutch, let out on it easy!" I begged for one more try and he let me, but he stood on the ground this time. I did it right this time and I was so proud!

He had bought cattle to raise for our own beef and he had bought some calves to raise so that we could sell them at auction for money. Our big momma cow named "Big Red" caught Pneumonia after giving birth to a calf and she couldn't recover. Daddy covered her with plastic to protect her from the cold rain and got her some antibiotics and gave her shots to help her get better. He had to teach me how to take care of her while he was gone for the week, so he taught me how to feed and water her from my hand and how to give her the daily shots. I went faithfully every evening after school. One day, I went out barefooted (which wasn't unusual for us country kids) to run down to take care of Bid Red, but as I was running, I jumped across the creek and my foot landed on a piece of broken cement pipe, that cut my foot really bad. I just took a piece of a rag and wrapped it around my foot and went on out to take care of her cause I knew that she and my Daddy were depending on me. I took responsibility to heart because I knew that my Daddy appreciated it. It got me lots of positive attention!

I was a good farm hand. I knew how to feed the cattle and feed the baby calves. By the way, Big Red's baby calf was raised by Bud and me. We bottle fed him until he was big enough to go to grain. Daddy promised Bud that when he was full grown, he would take him to auction to sell him for Bud to open a savings account. I was angry because I did most of the work, but Daddy promised that the next calf would be mine.

He went to auction as promised and sold our baby (now full grown) but he also bought a bunch of other baby calves for us to raise. He gave me first pick of which one would be mine to raise and sell, and I picked out the cutest black calf with white boots, so I named him "Boots". We bought several buckets with nipples on them and Daddy hung a rail in the barn to hang all the buckets on in the little stalls. We could feed them in two shifts. There were 15 calves. Daddy taught us how to mix the powdered milk for a near full bucket instead of the little calf bottle we had used before. It was so much fun. The little calves would butt at the bucket to make it work faster and the milk would slosh out on their faces. They would back up a second and then go back for more. It was a lot of hard work but we didn't know that. To us, we were having fun AND making money!

A few weeks later, our calves were growing up but Daddy noticed that some of them looked sick. He called the Veterinarian out to the house and he confirmed that they had caught a dreadful disease. It was "Pink-eye". Daddy told me and I told him that Pink-eye wasn't so bad, I had it before, but Daddy explained that it was deadly for cattle. The Vet gave him some purple medicine to put in their eyes several times a day and Daddy in turn taught Bud and me how to administer the medicine. He was very careful to explain how important it was that we take care of them while he was gone. When he returned the next weekend, the Vet returned and told him to destroy the sick ones and sell the others before they contracted it. Daddy did as the vet told him. One of the sick ones was Boots. I cried and cried. I really loved my calf. I was already used to Daddy having to destroy cattle when they were beyond hope, because he had to shoot Big Red and the other cow that had pneumonia. She had gotten stuck in a cold creek for days. I would always cry as Daddy would head out with his rifle. He told me what he had to do but he also told me that he wasn't going to let them suffer any longer. I wanted to go with him when he had to shoot Big Red but he told me stay at the house. I heard the gun go off and the tears streamed down.

By this time in my life, I had been trained in all the household chores except washing clothes. I had been washing dishes since I was 5 years old even though I had to stand in a chair to accomplish the task, but at 9 and 10 years old, I was trained in dusting, sweeping, mopping, vacuuming and cleaning the restrooms. A real Cinderella I was! Oh, I was not a stepchild and I knew by this age, that I was adopted, but to me that didn't make a difference, they were my real parents. Mother's duties were cooking and washing the clothes (this didn't include folding them - I had to help with that). I used to think that it was unfair that I had to do all the housecleaning, but I did get good training. I hated every moment of it though because I couldn't go out and play until it was all done and of course, if it weren't done right (to her satisfaction) then I had to start all over! Fridays were basically spent doing my chores. Sometimes, I would be finished by early afternoon.

Fifth grade was uneventful but sixth grade was not. First of all, we could be in the band in 6th grade and I already knew how to play the piano, so I decided to play the marching bells because I knew all the notes. I got to play all the other percussion instruments also, snare drum, triangle etc. It was great! We would also play for the 9th grade football game once or twice. I was doing very well with it and even practiced marching and could carry the bells without falling. I was so proud of myself. The very first football game for us to play, was finally announced by Mr. Bruton, and I took my note home to Mother. That note told what day the game was and what time we had to be there. It was at 7:00pm on a Thursday night and she didn't feel like driving all the way in to town for that, and so she told me that I couldn't go. Then I begged and pleaded and that didn't help, so then I asked her if I could get someone to come by and pick me up and she refused that as well. She wasn't going to allow me to put anyone out for me to go to some stupid football game. That was it. The end of my big band career before I even had a chance to begin. That was to be expected. See, had Bud not dropped out, then I could have been there. Some how, I did get to attend one of the football games in town, but not as a band player, just a fan in the stands.

During my sixth grade year, my Mother decided to go back to school to feel more fulfillment. She decided to enter LVN school. I was happy for her decision because I thought that it would do her good, to get out of the house, and be proud of herself. It wasn't an easy school for her. She had brought home tons of thick books to learn and we would have to be quiet while she studied. I would sit at the table often and look through her books. They were very interesting and I knew that I wanted to grow up and be a Doctor! She struggled to make decent grades. I went up to her school with her once and she showed me around. It was very exciting!

She got lots of new friends and began inviting them to our house for parties when Daddy was gone to work. She made Bud and I swear that we would never tell him because he would get mad at her. I know why he would too! Her friends were drinking. No, not water or cokes. They were drinking beer and whiskey and stuff. I knew that Daddy didn't like that and he didn't like smoking either, like they were doing in his house. Some of the people were listening to dirty records telling nasty jokes. Bud especially enjoyed that. I just kept trying to be a good hostess helper for Mother. Then I had to learn a few new tricks, like how to attempt to sober-up a passed out drunk. I learned that if you give them a concoction of something, that will make them throw up. I had the recipe for the concoction. It consisted of hot sauce and Worcestershire sauce and hot water and vegetable oil and some other nasty stuff. The trick is, to get a passed out drunk to drink. They tend to be oblivious to their surroundings. Well, we were able to get them to drink it and they did throw up. I don't know if it made them sober or not, but at least they were able to sit up and drink all the coffee. I had to clean up their vomit off the floor, but I really didn't mind because my Mother seemed to be proud of me for helping out so well.

When Daddy came home, he some how found out about her party. Boy, was he mad! I've never seen him this mad. He even tried to spank Mother for allowing a party like that in front of his children. I didn't want Mother to get into trouble because this was one of the first times that we were getting along. This was the only time that I ever saw him touch my mother and I was scared for her but he quickly got his control and just left the room. He wasn't a fighting type of father.

Mother began a new pattern after that party. She started taking little trips to a little liquor store that was several miles away. She didn't want anyone to see her buying the stuff because they might tell Daddy. She would leave me sitting in the car while she ran in to make her selections. When she would come out to the car, she would drink some of it and then hide the rest under the seat. She swore me to secrecy and of course, I would never tell a soul. I didn't want her mad at me. I really didn't know much about Vodka and liquor to know that there was anything really wrong with it but I had learned that people can sure throw up a lot after drinking too much!

This was the year that we sixth grade girls practiced for the Junior High Cheerleading tryouts. I was good at the cheers because I had a very strong loud voice. We always joked around that I never needed a megaphone, I came equipped! My only drawback was that I couldn't do a cartwheel. I tried very hard but I could only do a round-off. Hopefully that would be enough to make the team. This was actually my favorite event. I just had to make it!

This was the year that the girls in my class were all beginning to wear bras. That is, everyone but me and maybe one other girl. Even Melinda Pomykal was wearing one and she was just a skinny toothpick. It was very embarrassing for me but I felt that my time would come soon.

Sixth grade was also the most fun year because of what we were learning. In Science class we had to learn all of the bones in the body and I was the first to have them memorized. I was very good at all the Science work and my English/Spelling work. Those were my favorite subjects. I wasn't interested in History but I enjoyed Geography. I was pretty good at Math but not great. I usually made A/B Honor Roll. If I didn't make Honor Roll, then I had only missed it by only 1 or 2 points in one subject. I never really had to study to make good grades as long as I listened and did my work.

Just before the cheerleader tryouts, I was in my bedroom late at night and I was sitting up listening to the TV. I overheard a conversation between Mother and Daddy and they were discussing a divorce. I couldn't believe that they were actually talking seriously about this, but they were and they were even making the plans. They weren't yelling or screaming about it, just talking. They then decided to go to some counseling.

They went to a few sessions and every time they would come home they would discuss some of the Dr.'s suggestions. Once, Daddy said that he was a quack. I didn't know what that was at first but I figured it out in the context of their conversation. After a few of those sessions, they just agreed to discontinue any further sessions and go ahead and get the divorce. The were both pretty "matter of fact" about it. They didn't seem upset at all.

In the meantime, I was screaming with joy inside! I was going to get to live with Daddy and never have to be with her again. I knew that Bud would go to live with her since he was her pet. A few days later, Mother approached Bud and me together and asked Bud specifically, who he wanted to live with. He told Mother that he was going to have a hard time choosing but that he thought that it would be best if he went with Daddy because he was almost a teenager. He needed to be with a man. Well, I wasn't too upset until Mother spoke up and said, "Well Cathy, I guess that means that you go with me because whoever Bud chooses to go with, then Daddy and I agreed that you would go with the other". My life was over. How could I live apart from my Daddy and worst of all, how could I live with her! Bud's final decision was my worst nightmare. They put the house up for sale and made plans to move. Daddy told her that he would split up the household furnishings giving her the living room suit, master bedroom suite, and kitchen set, and my bedroom suite and he would take the dining set, guest bedroom suite and Bud's bedroom suite. I just couldn't believe how "matter of fact" they were about this.

Chapter 4: The move from home

This was all happening so fast. The house sold to the very first prospect. The prospective buyers fell in love at first sight. The house and land had always been the talk of the town, so it was no wonder that it sold immediately! They wanted to take over the home in 30 days and in 30 days or less, we were gone.

It seemed unusual that Mother and Daddy were getting along so well through this. He helped her to find an affordable apartment and even moved all our things and hooked up the washer and dryer. The apartment seemed nice and clean. It was a two bedroom and it had a playground close to our apartment. School was only a short walk across a field. There were quite a few kids that lived around this place, which was a bonus after living out in the boonies.

The new school would be an adventure. I had been in the same little country school for almost 6 years until now and I just kind of thought that everything would be the same, except for different faces and classrooms. Boy, was I in for a shock! This school population was about 85% Black people! Not that I had anything against them but I wasn't used to being around many of them. We only had two or three black students in the entire school at Troy and none were in my grade level so I never really associated with any before. I felt like a bleach spot in a sea of black ink! I really tried to make friends with my classmates and was fairly successful in just a few short days. I was a very friendly and outgoing girl that never met a stranger. Things went along well the first week.

On the first weekend, Mother decided to go out. She didn't have a sitter for me and didn't know anyone around there yet, so she decided to take me with her. She asked to get dressed up sort of nice and so I did. I was excited to go with her; I felt like her buddy. We went to a bar. I had never been to a bar before! It was dark and smoky inside and it had a jukebox playing country music. I liked country music because Mother would occasionally play it at home. There were several people inside but they were all adults. No children in sight. Not even a teenager! I sat at the table with Mother and she ordered a beer for herself and a Coke for me. We hadn't been there 5 minutes before some old man came to the table and started up a conversation with Mother. She introduced me to him and he commented on what a pretty girl I was and how much I looked like my mother. (If they only knew!) People always told us that we looked alike. Later on, he asked her to dance and then later on, he asked her if he could dance with me. I think that he was just trying to be nice. I couldn't dance at all, but he said that he could teach me. I was always taught to try new things and not to be rude to people, so I accepted. I probably looked like an idiot out there, stepping all over his boots, but he stayed with it until the song was over. I thought it was kind of fun, but I felt out of place and uneasy. The man danced a few more times with Mother and we went home fairly early. Mother thanked me for being good.

Monday came and it was back to school. At the end of the day, I got a notice that the principal wanted to see me in his office after school. I thought that there was probably some transfer paper work left undone so I wasn't the least bit worried. When the bell rang, I went right on up to the front office and told them that I was there. This Principal was a man that I knew from our church that we attended in Troy. I had to wait for a short while and finally his door opened. Some parents and another student walked out and he called me in and asked me to shut the door.

He started off by asking me how things were going and I told him that things were fine. He asked me if I was having any problems with any students and I told him that there were no problems. I was waiting for him to give me the papers that he needed to have filled out but he kept asking over and over if there were any problems at all with any of the students. He let me know that I could talk to him about it if there were and I assured him that there were none! He asked me to sit down and he asked me why my classmate would tell him that I were calling her names. I asked, "Who?" He didn't want to mention any names and then turned and asked me again why a student would tell him that I was calling her a bad name. I told him that I didn't know what he was talking about and so he told me that I could go home. He never told me anything more.

I went home and told Mother what had happened and she started drilling me with the same questions. I finally made her understand that the principal must have misunderstood this student and they must have been talking about some other student.

The next day at school seemed normal. Every thing went as usual until the last period of the day, I got another note saying that I was to go to the office after the bell. This time I was a little more concerned, but I knew that I hadn't done anything wrong so I didn't worry too much.

I went in to the office as directed and the principal was waiting for me. He asked me to close the door again and to have seat. He again asked me why I had a student telling him that I was calling her bad names. I couldn't believe that we were back to this again. I told him that I wasn't calling anyone any names and then told him that if he would just let me know what I was being accused of, then maybe I would have some kind of explanation. He finally told me what was reported to him. My classmate - Cathy Jewel - told him that I was calling her a dirty name. I told him that I had never called her any names at all and that he would just have to believe me because I was innocent! He insisted that there had to be something to it for her to come to him two days in a row and report this to him. He didn't think that she should have any reason to lie about it. I then talked frankly with him and said, "You've known me a long time from church and you should know that I wouldn't sit here and lie to you. Now, if you want to tell me what she is claiming that I'm calling her, maybe I have, and I'm just not aware." He thought that this was a logical request and so he told me. He said that she told him that I was calling her a "black slut". I had no idea what he was talking about. I told him that I had never called her that and that I didn't even know what it was! I asked him to explain what it was and that maybe I had said it in some other way not knowing that it was wrong. (You see, I came from a very "country" school and kids never said words like that. I knew very few curse words. I guess you could say that we were naive.) Anyway, he finally believed me that I hadn't called her that, but he gave me a very stiff warning! He told me that I needed to be careful. He said that I shouldn't walk out on the streets alone around there because he had reports from junior high boy's parents telling him how she had beat them up and they were even bigger than she was. He said that she must be jealous for some reason and just trying to get me into trouble. That comment sparked a thought! She had made a comment in class one day, that she didn't like my name and that her name was "Cathy Jewel" and to make sure that I called her that! So he must have been right, she must be jealous that we have the same name (nearly)! He even suggested that I walk to and from school with other kids so I wouldn't be alone. He cautioned me to steer clear of her!

I took the caution to heart and went straight home and told Mother what had happened. She was angry that this had happened and she called Daddy and asked him to help her find another place to live. He was there that weekend, and helped her to buy a Mobile Home and to get it set up in a Mobile Home Park not too far away, but definitely in a different school district. By Tuesday the next week, I was enrolling in a new school!

As soon as I got home from school that day, I went walking around the Mobile Home Park to see what was around there. I went down to the Recreation room by the swimming pool and went inside and saw that they had a pool table and a Ping-Pong table and "MELISSA! What are you doing here?!" "I live here!" she exclaimed. Then she asked me what I was doing there and I told her that I lived there too! Melissa Annette Wiley had been my very, very, very best friend at Troy until her parents moved away at the beginning of the school year. I was crushed when she had moved away and thought that life couldn't go on without her and this was just too great! We were back together!

Now that Mother was working full time, I had a lot of free time to be on my own. I wasn't really on my own though, I was with Melissa. We found lots of stuff to do and we even found Charles' phone number. He was a boy that I used to like in the 5 grade at Troy and he also had moved away and was now living only a few blocks away. We talked on the phone mostly because he lived outside of the park area, but there were a few times that we would go over there. Sometimes we would talk on the phone 'till late at night, even after midnight if Mother wasn't home yet or she was in her room and didn't know.

Mother began liking this young man that she had met at the bar. I didn't go with her much anymore, because I would always prefer to stay with Melissa. This guy had a weird name - Funkenbush! He acted like he was really in love with her and me and he asked her to marry him just a few weeks after they met. He took us to his parent's home in Belton to meet them and announced their intent to marry. I didn't care one way or the other. I thought that it was too soon and too quick but I was just a kid, what did I know? I felt that if this man would make her happy, then I was accepting of the idea. After all, he was very, very nice to me.

It was only a week later that they got married and he moved in with us. He had been living with his parents, I guess, so he was eager to get things done. They were married only a short time when he and I clashed on a few things. He tried to tell me that I couldn't do something that Mother had already given me permission to do and I let him know real quick that he wasn't my Daddy! Mother made me apologize to him for that statement and the two of them went off to discuss the matter.

A few days later, Mother told me that they were getting an annulment. "A what?" I asked. An annulment. She explained that it was kind of like a divorce, but it means that the marriage never counted since they were together for only a month. Oh well! I had gotten to the point that I didn't like him anyway and Mother told me that she thought that he had married her for me. I didn't understand that until she mentioned Uncle Don liking young girls and she said that he had made a few comments about my long pretty legs and she didn't want anything to do with him after that. I was very glad to hear her explanation. It made me understand that she wasn't just getting **too** loose. She was already doing a lot of things since she and Daddy divorced that I didn't approve of, such as, drinking and smoking and sleeping with men. She didn't do it where I would see what was going on, but I wasn't blind and stupid either. If I knocked on the door and heard two people whispering and she was telling me to go away from the door and go play, then I knew that she was trying to get rid of me so that I wouldn't know that a man was in her room and she could give him chance to sneak out. I wasn't very proud of her, to say the least!

It wasn't too much longer before she found a new boyfriend from another visit to the bar. He wasn't a real hot catch either. When we went to visit him at his house, we just saw a dirty, run down little place that had only the bare essentials in it. His bed didn't even have a bedspread. It was just a set of springs and a mattress on top with one sheet that wasn't even fitted to the mattress. It was apparent that he was not into success. I couldn't believe that she would even consider a man like this after Daddy. She wasn't accustomed to trashy man or lifestyles.

A few more months passed and then Mother got a call from her sister in Abilene - Aunt Faye - saying that their mother wasn't doing well, who is my Granny S. She said that Granny was going to have to be placed into a nursing home. Since Mother had her LVN license, she then decided that it would be best that we move to Abilene so that she could get a job at the nursing home where her mother was and that way she could help out and be near her. This wasn't the kind of news that was going to make me happy. I didn't want to go that far away from my Daddy, who had found an apartment in Waco, nor did I want to leave my best friend - Melissa - again. I was just getting used to this new place and my new school and meeting new friends.

Well, she had made up her mind and we were going. She found a Mobile Home Park called Gateway, that wasn't far from the nursing home and she had our trailer home moved up their. Well, that was certainly easier than packing and moving, but I still wasn't very happy.

When we got there, I looked all around to see if there were any kids my age, and to see what this park had to offer. The front part of the park was very pretty. The homes has pretty grass and trees and there was a nice office at the front with a nice pool. There wasn't much of a recreation room though. It was only equipped with a few chairs and a couch and was kept locked. This was also where we got our mail. We lived at the end of the park where there were not very many trailers and there was no grass or trees, only weeds. It was always my job to mow the yard and it was very difficult to mow over all the rocks. Mother didn't have the money to have a nice yard installed so we made do with weeds.

I found a girl that was my age named Terry. She had dark, coarse, auburn hair that was long, right past her shoulders. She was about my size, so we could trade off clothes and to 12 year old girls, that was very important! We became very good friends. She helped me find my way around the new school, but I wasn't really interested in knowing too much about the elementary school because this was the end of April, and in 6 weeks school we would be out and would be going to Lincoln Jr. High School in the fall.

Terry and I had plenty of time to spend together because Mother worked until late in the evenings most of the time. Mother didn't really care what I did as long as I did my chores and stayed out of trouble. My chores seemed a lot easier since we lived in a 14 X 60' mobile home that had 2 bedrooms and one bath and 1 living area. It was all much easier to clean. Oh! We had carpet! It's much easier to vacuum than to sweep and mop tile floors. Our mobile home had beautiful red curtains with red and black fringe and they were tied back to see the black sheers. Our carpet was a beautiful red and black shag. It all went great with our black vinyl furniture! Everyone that visited commented on our pretty house. Cleaning the whole house only took me about 2 - 3 hours each week and that was nothing compared to our home in Troy.

It was during this summer that I took up smoking. Mother smoked and always kept her carton in the kitchen pantry so it was very easy to sneak out a pack. A pack lasted us for a month because we rarely had the courage to light them up because they made us nauseous and our heads would spin so badly that we could hardly walk straight for a while, but if we looked cool and older, it would be worth it!

We occasionally would walk across the street to the Westgate Mall and look around. Neither of us ever had any money, but we could still pass the time, by going in and trying things on and pretending that we could get them. One day we had been in a store trying on sunglasses and just dying laughing at how funny we looked in some of them, when all of a sudden a man came and took me by the arm and told me and Terry to follow him to the store office! I didn't know whether to trust him or not to take us to the store office. I was also confused why he would even have a reason to take us to the office if we were being truthful! I asked him what was going on and why he was taking us with him and he was quite abrupt and told me that we would discuss it when we got to the office. Thank goodness it was only a short walk because I was really nervous! When we got in there, he sat down in his big chair in this tiny little office where there were two or three black and white TV screens where you could see the shoppers. He told us that he was Security and that he wanted the sunglasses back. I told him that the sunglasses were on the rack as I then understood that he was accusing us of stealing! How dare he! I asked him if it was against the law to try on sunglasses and he said the trying them on was not, but he seemed to be irritated by my retort. He asked us again where the sunglasses were and I again told him that I didn't have any sunglasses and I then looked at Terry, wondering if she had lifted a pair. When he and I looked at her, she immediately denied having any and I could tell that she was serious and telling the truth. I then asked him why he thought that we stole some and he pointed toward one of the monitoring TV screens and showed me the sunglass rack. He then said that he saw me pull a tag off the sunglasses and throw it on the floor and that as I stepped around the sunglass rack away from camera view for a moment I must have hid them because they weren't in my hands when I stepped back. Well! The stupidity of that man! Was placing them back on the rack not a reasonable option?! Then he starts asking us if we knew what a juvenile record was and started telling us that we're kind of young to start our lives with a police record and then he asked me again where I put the sunglasses. I guess that he thought that I was lying to him and that the part about the record would scare me into telling him the truth. I told him that I remembered a tag falling off one pair of sunglasses and that when I tried to put it back on the pair that it had fallen from, I found that it was broken and wouldn't stay on and I also insisted that the plastic string had to have already been broken before I picked them up because I didn't pull on it, it just fell off onto the floor. He didn't believe me, can you believe that?! Well this man had no clue that he had just crossed the one area that I had the most difficult time dealing with and that was, TO BE ACCUSED OF DOING SOMETHING THAT I DIDN'T DO! When he told me that he knew that I had them, I asked him if he would like to search my purse to prove that I didn't have them. He told me that searching my purse wouldn't be necessary and I got mad and dumped the contents out onto his desk saying, "SEE! I DON'T HAVE YOUR STUPID GLASSES! NOW DO YOU BELIEVE ME?" Well, he never admitted that he was wrong, but instead took our names and addresses and phone numbers and said that he would be calling us if they found out anything further. Then he told us that we were free to go. I was livid!!! He didn't even apologize!!! I turned to him and demanded an apology and he would only say that IF he WAS wrong, then he was sorry. We had to settle for those lame terms of regret and left swearing that we would never shop there again! (We never had any money anyway, so it was really no great loss for them.)

When we got to my house, I told Mother about the rude man at the store and she doubted me as well, but, when I told her that I had gotten angry and dumped my purse out to prove it, then she believed me a little more, but I could tell that she wasn't convinced. I had never stolen anything in my life except for that pack of cigarettes in the pantry.

A few weeks later, my Aunt Faye and Uncle George came by to visit and they spent the night with us. This visit was to meet Mother's new husband - Lee Wright. Granny had already passed away only a few months ago, so they talked about that and looked at pictures. Uncle Sonny had also come up to visit us from Waco since Aunt Faye was in town. They were brothers and sisters. Uncle Sonny was one of my favorite uncles because he was always nice to me. That night, we stayed up late playing Canasta and Rummy. He and I were partners and we kept winning! He was a great teacher.

The next morning, I woke up very early, about 6:00am and daylight had not yet dawned. I had an idea! Since everyone was still asleep, I snuck over to the cabinet where Aunt Faye had stored her purse to see if it was still in there. There it was! I was curious to see if there was any money in her wallet. When I opened the wallet, I saw a $5.00 bill and a $20.00 bill. I began to walk the path of true temptation. I thought to myself, "Surely she wouldn't miss a little ol' $5 bill, would she. No. Surely not. And I could really use it next time we went to the mall."

Then I did it! I took her money! I couldn't believe that I was doing this and I was terrified of being caught, but I carried out the final phase. I had to hide the money in my stuff so that no one would know. I quickly and quietly slipped it into my purse and laid back down on the couch, where I had been sleeping, to dream about how I would spend my new found fortune. This time I could shop for real!

I had always tried to earn my own spending money by mowing lawns, but I seldom got anyone to let me. I don't know if it was because I was a girl or what. I didn't even get an allowance.

That very evening, I was called in to the house by Mother to answer a few questions. I didn't like the sound of her voice when she called me.

I innocently asked her what she needed and she asked me to sit down at the kitchen table with her and Lee. She then told me that Aunt Faye was missing $5.00 in her billfold of her purse and asked if I had taken it. I explained that it was hard to believe that she would know exactly how much she had and that maybe she had forgotten that she spent it or miscounted. Mother then told me that she could tell that I was lying and wanted to know where the money was. Even though I lied a lot (to keep out of trouble), I was never very good at it. I could look her straight in the eye and lie and she still knew (or she was just a convincing guesser). I finally admitted to stealing her money and Mother told me that she had made arrangements for me since she couldn't handle me anymore.

What?!!! What could she be talking about? I never gave her any problems and she didn't even know about me trying out smoking. This was the only thing that I had done wrong!!! She said that she had called and found a girl's home for me to live in that could deal with me. She said that she was just tired of trying and maybe they could handle me. I was speechless.

I went to my room and cried and tried to sort things out. Did she really feel that she seriously couldn't deal with me (this was hard to believe since she was never home and just let me run around with Terry all the time) or was she just trying to get rid of me since she had a new husband?

Well, she was serious about their decision and it was only a few days before a lady, took me to a real girl's home. This lady was my case-worker. The place was a normal two-story house on the outside, but inside there were many bedrooms and several girls. There was a family that lived in the back area called the house parents. The lady was in a wheel chair and seemed pretty nice and the couple appeared to be in the late 30's. They had a little 5 or 6 year old boy and they all lived in the back two rooms on the main floor. There were two other bedrooms on the main floor at the front of the house and an upstairs bedroom and bath as well. This was where I would stay, upstairs. It was nice that there were fewer to share this bathroom since there were only three of us up there and there were another eight or nine sharing rooms downstairs. We all had bunk beds to sleep on and there were 2 empty ones in our room for newcomers. They had just lost a couple of girls prior to my arrival. I didn't ask where they went. I didn't really want to know right then how much worse things could get. They had mentioned a home in Gainesville Girl's Prison and that was more information than I had needed to hear right then. I wondered what these girls had done to end up here. Had they just stolen $5.00 from their Aunt's purse?

I unpacked my things into my chest of drawers and sat for a while to look around. You can learn a lot about someone just by looking around in their room. The posters told me some, their messy or neat bed and table tops told me more and the clothes in the closet told me even more. The case-worker came up to see if I had unpacked and she took me and introduced me to the other girls. I only got their names. A few of them spoke and smiled, and some just looked and turned their head in disinterest. They were all ages up to seventeen. I was the youngest, being 12, and there was one girl that was 13 named Theresa. She soon told me that she was glad that I came, because they always picked on her because she was the youngest and no one hung out with her. She seemed nice but I never could find out why she was there. She was my roommate. All the older girls said that she was a big baby. My other roomy was a Hispanic girl named Anna and she was fifteen and little bit over weight. She had long beautiful black hair. I felt very sorry for her because she said that her mother had left her and she was waiting for her to come back and get her. I asked her when she was going to come back and she said that she didn't know. She said that she had been there for nearly two years. She asked me why I was there and when I told her she laughed but apologized quickly explaining that she couldn't believe that I was there for that. She told me about the other girls and why they were there. They had either been habitual runaways, thieves or had too many fights etc. They were all in there for serious things, outright crimes. I was beginning to feel a bit out of place.

At least I was still going to the same school. I was even keeping up my grades. The case-worker told me that if I kept up my grades and stayed out of trouble, then I could get extra privileges.

Well, I soon learned the routine of the house. Everyone had chores to do and the chores rotated from week to week. I was not on the list for the first week (this was just my get acquainted week) but they had several categories. Floor duties, cooking duties, kitchen cleaning duties, bathroom duties. It didn't seem too bad to me because the workload was shared. It took me no time to finish my chores when I got them. They were even fun when I got to actually work along side someone else. Especially the cooking, Mother had never taught me how to cook. She had always told me to get lost.

Another plus to this new home were the boys. Yes, this was a girl's home but the boys definitely knew where it was. They always came by to visit the girls and the girls could even date as long they were of age and were not on any restrictions. Several guys had to stop by and see the new girl and several of them were very nice. Ther was an eighteen year old boy that I really had a crush on and he even asked me to go steady. Of course, I accepted. Just think of the prestige of telling all the other girls that my boyfriend was seven-teen!!!

It was Thanksgiving now and my Daddy was coming to pick me up for a short visit. I was so excited to see him. He came to the girl's home to get me and I was the happiest person in the world. He couldn't understand why Mother put me in this place. He was actually mad when he realized what kind of place it was, but he said that he didn't think that she would ever give him custody of me. I told him how she and her husband drank all the time, and he only said that he couldn't do anything to change that but was sorry that I was having to go through that kind of stuff. Our visit was too short. It was over as fast as it had begun, but he promised to come back and get me for Christmas.

When I returned from my visit with Daddy, I tried to get in touch with my boyfriend but found that he was seeing some other girl. That was a crushing blow!

Feeling at a total loss, I sought attention by desperate means. I made a suicide attempt! I really didn't want to die, I just wanted people to know how much pain I felt. I missed my Daddy desperately, apparently my mother shoved me into this home to get rid of me and I was the new target of being picked on and beat up since I was the youngest. My family had forbade me to ever come around since they didn't believe that I was truthful about Uncle D, and now I lost my boyfriend! Didn't anyone love me or care that I couldn't cope with anything else. Twelve year old girls aren't suppose to know how to deal with these things, are they? If so, then I wasn't taught how. The only assistance I was receiving was some counseling time with my case-worker. I wasn't sure exactly how much I could say to her. I made the attempt by trying to slice my wrist. I had a razor-blade and kept trying to slice it, but I couldn't do it right because it hurt so much. The more I thought about my actions, the more I knew that ending my life WOULD be the best thing. At least I would be out of everybody's hair. I tried several times making the cuts a little deeper each time but not getting enough pressure. This was too hard! I decided to try something else instead. I looked for pills in the medicine cabinet but they were all locked up downstairs with the house parents. Then I noticed the heater! It was a gas wall heater and I knew that this would be much easier. All I had to do was turn on the gas and I could just go to sleep, FOREVER! It was very simple. I just turned the valve on and sat in the floor and took time to think. I also took a moment to pray to ask God to forgive me for wanting to die and doing something so stupid. I realized that I was beginning to get very sleepy and someone then knocked on the door. I got scared that someone might figure out what I was doing so I opened the door and ran! I ran out of the bathroom , the bedroom, down the stairs, out the front door and down the street and hid in some bushes. I realized that people would probably figure out what I was doing and they would take me to a nut house. Soon, I saw people coming down the street and heard them talking about me. They began calling out my name - "CATHY! CATHY!" The people had all left the area, at least I thought so, but I was mistaken. One of the older girl's boyfriends named Bill was still standing around out of my view, and when I came out of the bushes and saw him, I began to run! I was not successful this time. He caught me! Instead of him dragging me immediately down to the home, he sat me down and talked to me and asked me what was wrong. I sat and cried on his shoulder for about fifteen minutes telling him all about my problems and he said that he understood. Wow! I couldn't believe that he also felt things were bad for me and I wasn't just a baby that couldn't handle things. He also encouraged me to hang in there and told me that I was too pretty to throw myself away because some stupid guy dumped me for those kind of reasons. I felt more assured hearing this from another eighteen year old guy. I got my composure and he walked me back to the house.

The house mother didn't demand to speak with me, but just offered to if I wanted. I really wasn't in the mood right then but thanked her and went to my room.

It was only a few days later, that I had run across a really cute guy who was interested in me, but this time he was my age. We hung out together a lot and even did homework together at the park or outside on the front lawn. He was really nice. His name was Stephen.

As the next couple of weeks passed, I had further meetings with my case-worker and I learned that she had heard about my stupid stunt. She told me that she was concerned about me and wanted to know what I thought that I needed. I didn't know what to say but I did tell her that I was getting beat up and picked on a lot by the older girls. Even Theresa joined in the teasing. I guess that Theresa felt more accepted by the others if she did. The case-worker said that she was going to see what she could do about making some changes but she didn't give me any hints about what that might be.

Only a few days after this conversation with the case-worker the older girls were beginning to be really nice to me and treating me like a little sister. They even loaned me some of their clothes sometimes and fixed me up with make-up and did my hair. They even taught me how to dance. We were right in the middle of dancing in the den one evening when the door bell rang, and my case-worker walked in. I wasn't expecting her and went to ask her why she was there. She told me that I needed to pack my things by tomorrow afternoon because she was taking me to another place to live. This wasn't good news. I knew that I had told her only a week ago that I was having a lot of difficulties but now they were being nice to me. I wasn't ready to leave and I wasn't sure what the next place would be like. I went on up and packed all my things and then I went to bed in tears. Anna overheard me and came and held me in my bed until I went to sleep.

My case-worker came to pick me up from school early the next day to take me to my new place. She wanted a chance to talk to me about the new home and how this would be different from the last. She told me that I would be in a Foster home with a family that had six other children. The oldest boy living there was also 12 years old and he was a Foster child like I was. His name was Chip. The other 5 children were their natural children. She told me that they were a really nice family and that she thought that this arrangement would be better for me because I would be the oldest here. I listened to her logic and even though she expressed how she was trying to help me, I didn't really want to make this change. The day was a Friday and I later learned that the day was chosen intentionally so that the family could all be together for the weekend and I could get to know them better. The first night was basically simple formal greetings and unpacking. I was trying to familiarize myself with my surroundings. Basically, little kids everywhere. They were in age range from 6 months to 9 years. I enjoyed talking to Chip. He said that he had been living there for almost a year and that the family was OK but that he didn't really like watching after the kids. That next night was family night. I didn't know what family night was and they explained to me that the family gets together every Saturday evening to play games together and that since this was my first weekend with their family, they would give me the choice of game to play. Well, that was nice of them and we had a nice time playing the game together and that is when they told me that the next morning we were going to Church. I liked church and had gone faithfully at the girl's home and even when I lived with Mother. No! She didn't take me. I always rode the church bus. It was nice that they would come to pick me up every Sunday.

I asked the family what church we would be going to and they told me this really long name that I didn't really understand and when they saw that I was puzzled, they told me that they were Mormons. I didn't know what a Mormon was but as long as they go to church then that must be OK!

I met a new boy that lived in the neighborhood and he drove a pretty blue fastback car. I wasn't sure what kind it was, but the color was very pretty. For a 12 year old girl, the name of the car wasn't important as long as it looked cool! He was cute too. He was seventeen years old. Well, that was cool. He is old enough to tell all the girls about AND he has a car. He came over to visit me often at the street in front of my house. He would park there and we would sit out on the hood and talk for hours. He was really nice. I soon learned that all older boys had one thing on their minds though. SEX! I had to turn down the last guy several times and now this guy was starting in. He soon realized that I wasn't about to do something like that and so he dumped me. Not again! I couldn't handle this again, so soon after the last one. Once again, I attempted suicide. I didn't have the nerve to follow through with swallowing any more aspirins and I stopped after about 8 of them. It was enough to make my ears ring tremendously and so I went to bed early and decided to cry myself to sleep instead.

I learned what Chip meant about watching after the kids. I felt like the new live-in babysitter. She was always asking me to look after one or two of them, but I really didn't like doing this. I didn't know how to make kids mind. Then there was that screaming baby! I just couldn't bear to hear that baby cry! I yelled at it and told it to shut up but he just cried all the louder. I finally got tired of dealing with him and told him that if he didn't shut up, then I was going to leave him in his crib. I was sure that after yelling and warning him of the crib, that he would surely SHUT UP, but he continued at a maddening state. That did it!!! I went over and shook the baby and threw him in his crib and walked out of the room. I walked into the kitchen to think for a minute and then I would feel sorry for him and so I went back to pick him up and soon as he saw me, he started screaming again. I begged him to stop and finally resorted to setting him back in his crib to cry alone. I finally broke down and gave him a bottle to help him to stop crying even though it was not his scheduled feeding time. That worked! He was now willing to lie in his crib and drink his bottle quietly, and eventually he fell asleep. Thank goodness she came home before he awoke.

A few days later, this family went to visit some of their friends. We drove out to some country home and while we were there, I got very depressed. I felt like I didn't belong there. I wasn't part of their family no matter how I tried to look at it and I just could take anymore.

I went down to ask the lady of the house if I could use her telephone. She saw tears in my eyes and asked if everything was alright. I told her that I would just like to call my Mother and she said that the phone call might help me.

When I called Mother, she sounded strange. She didn't sound drunk but her speech was slurred and she was very depressed. I asked her if I could please come home. I even promised that I would never do anything to upset her again and especially steal! I begged and pleaded and told her that I just needed to be home and that I would help her with anything.

She was quiet for a moment, and began crying. She said that she didn't really know what to do with me because she couldn't even figure out what to do for herself. She said that she and Lee weren't getting along very well and she didn't know if she could handle me at home too. I didn't tell her that I had attempted to end my life a few times, but I did tell her that I did not like being with another family and that I didn't belong there. I told her that I belonged with her. I assured her that I could really help her if she would just let me come home and before I hung up, she promised that she would consider it and check into it.

Well, I wasn't going to hold my breath while waiting for her final decision so I tried to carry on as normal as possible. It didn't matter how hard I tried, it just didn't seem right.

Now two weeks had passed. My case-worker was going to try to cheer me by enrolling me in some ballet and dance classes. She thought that this would really help me out and so she picked me up from school and took me to pick out the shoes and sign up. Wow! A bright spot in my life! Maybe I would be really good at this! I took my new shoes home as though they were a treasure. I put them on and showed them to Chip and to my foster mother. Chip thought they were dumb, but the foster mother was encouraging.

The next day, the case-worker returned to the foster house after I had come home from school. I knew this wasn't the day that she had told me my dance classes would be so what kind of surprise would this be?

She was there to tell me that I was going home. She was there to help me to pack and take me to Mother's house. What terrible timing! I never dreamed that I would have had the opportunity to take dance lessons but I did want to go home too. Now the dance lessons would be out for sure. The case worker asked me to give the dance and ballet shoes to her and she would return them to the store. She told me that she was glad that I could be with my mother and hoped that everything would work out well.

The first evening at home went well. I got into bed that night and thanked God for helping me to be able to come home. Mother and Lee were still awake and in the kitchen. I hadn't been in bed long when they started arguing over something. I wasn't sure what it was all about, but I stayed awake for a while to listen and to make sure that everything would be OK. Their voices got louder and louder and they were using a lot of curse words. Mother called him a "lazy S.O.B." and he got mad and I yelled and then I heard something break up and a thump on the floor! I jumped out of bed to see what was happening and Mother was screaming and bleeding by her eye and then she turned and told me while still yelling and crying, " That lousy thing just hit me in the eye with his hot tea. He scalded the shit out me and..." She stopped yelling for a moment and touched her eyebrow. Then, she looked at her hand and found blood on it. Lee walked out of the kitchen and into the bedroom. I went over and gave Mother a hug and asked her to sit down while I ran to get some bandages. They had been drinking quite heavily just an hours earlier, but they had been getting along fine until this. Drinking surely does cause their moods to change quickly. I got the bandages and medicine to doctor her wound. She seemed glad that I was helping her and she started talking to me about how she had obviously made another mistake. I asked her what kind of mistake she was talking about and she said that she meant in picking a husband. She told me that this old louse was just after her for her money and a free ride. She told me how useless he was and that he didn't want to work, he just sat at home messing up the house and drinking and smoking all day, expecting her to support his lazy self.

I didn't know what to say so I just listened and told her that I loved her and that everything would be OK. She didn't agree with me but she did thank me for helping her clean up. She was heading back toward the bedroom and I was so afraid that they would get into another fight so I followed right behind her. He was passed out in the bed and still holding a lit cigarette. Mother walked toward her bed (they had twin beds) on the other side and went over and took the cigarette from between his fingers and put it out. She then made a comment that he was going to wind up burning the house down sometime by always falling asleep smoking. She showed me a spot on his mattress that had already been charred by a previous burn that she just happened to catch before it got out of control. By this time, it was 2:00am and I needed to get to sleep so I could wake up for school the next day.

I was very proud of myself for helping her out as I had promised to do and I even felt needed.

6:30am came quickly. I wasn't able to fall asleep until 2:30 am that night because I wanted to make sure that she was asleep too before I did. So with only four hours of sleep, I moved rather slowly. I almost missed the bus, but managed to run really fast and catch it. Terry asked me why I looked so bad that morning and so I told her all about last nights episode.

That evening I helped Mother out by cooking them a very special dinner. I had never used this recipe before. Mother and Lee both commented on how wonderful it was and Mother even admitted that she couldn't take the credit for my new skills. She asked me where I had learned to cook and I told her that I had to help out in those other homes. I told her that I really enjoyed cooking!

She and Lee began celebrating early in the evening. I don't know what they had to celebrate, except that they seemed to be getting along better, but I don't know that they ever needed an excuse to celebrate. Drinking was just what they did. It only seemed that they were beginning earlier than usual.

Later on, by around 11:00pm, they began arguing again, this time it was about whether he was going to go find a job tomorrow or not. They were yelling and screaming and only throwing sarcasms this time. By 1:30 am, I stepped in and asked them to go to bed. They thought it was funny that I was telling/asking them to go to bed. Lee made a smart comment to me and Mother told me to get the belt and whip his butt for smarting off. She told me that she was serious, she wanted the belt.

They were both totally drunk and acting like little kids so when I returned to the living room with the belt, I took charge. I told them both that I needed to make sure that they were going to be OK and that I wanted them to go to bed right now, "PLEASE!" I pleaded. They were humored by this and de-cided to head for bed. They were going to take their drinks with them, but I told them that they had both had enough and to leave them there. I told them that I would clean up the living room, just go on to bed. Again, they were humored and complied. As they crawled into bed, I went down to make sure that everything was going to be alright and that there were no lit cigarettes. Lee had lit one up and so I showed him the belt and threatened to spank him if he didn't put the cigarette out and lay down and go to sleep. He laughed at me, but did as I asked. Mother laughed too and soon, they were both asleep. I had the living room cleaned up by 2:00am and this time I fell asleep by 2:15am.

The next morning, I had a more difficult time getting up, but managed again. Terry was quite amused with the story about my night last night. She couldn't believe that I had the belt this time. School work seemed harder that day because I never seemed to wake up. At least the day before that, I was fine by the time I got to school. This was a very long day and I was eager to get home so I could take a short nap.

Well, that was out of the question, because Lee hadn't gone out to get a job after all. He was there as usual, sitting at the kitchen table, drinking and smoking. I didn't feel comfortable to go to sleep. Mother came home from work and I helped her with supper. She wasn't very happy with Lee this evening because he didn't go to the Unemployment Office as he had promised. During dinner, they argued back and forth about his ability to find a job and all. After Mother and I cleaned up the kitchen, she went somewhere for an hour but had taken a few drinks before she left.

When she returned, she took a few more drinks (of hard liquor - not beer) and went into her bathroom. Lee was in the bedroom with the big liquor bottle back there, so he didn't need to come out for refills, he could just stay back there and drink without bothering anyone. I heard Mother rummaging through the medicine cabinet in the bathroom. I didn't know what she was doing, but I could hear most everything through the thin mobile home walls. The bathroom was right in between her back bedroom and my bedroom. My bedroom was also next to the kitchen. I was in my room on the phone with Terry for about 30 minutes. Mother finally came out of the bathroom and went to the kitchen for another drink and then went and sat on the living room couch. After about 15 more minutes, Mother called me into the living room. She said that she needed to talk to me.

She started off telling me about how she just couldn't get it together and how she was so very unhappy with Lee and she didn't know how she could carry on any longer. She told me that I could call Aunt Faye or my Dad and live with them when she was gone. I asked her what she meant and where she was going to go? She looked at me for a few minutes with a very blank, dazed look. I asked her again. She then told me that she was ready to die. I told her that she was too young to die and she said that she couldn't take anymore and then her speech got really slurred and I asked her what was wrong with her. I was getting really scared and then she told me that she had taken several of Lee's heart pills and that it was too late to help her. I barely understood what she was trying to say and then she passed out and fell in the floor. I tried to wake her up and realized that I needed to get her some help! I ran to her bedroom and was telling Lee that Mother had committed suicide and that I needed him to help her!!! He just sat there, looked at me, and said, "I'm not doing a damn thing for that bitch!" I begged and pleaded for him to help her and he just sat there! Well, I wasn't going to wait for him to move, so I got on the telephone and called Aunt Faye. I was crying and trying to tell her what had happened and she told me to hang up, call the ambulance and that she and Uncle George would be there shortly!!!

I called the ambulance and told them that my Mother had overdosed on heart medication and the lady on the phone asked me if she was still alive. I put the phone down, ran and checked to see and found that she was still breathing, but barely!!! The lady assured me that the medic would be there soon and she asked me to find the pill bottle that Mother had taken the pills from.

I ran into the bathroom and found the bottle opened on the counter. There were just a few left in the bottle!

The ambulance arrived very quickly! I had been sitting, holding her while waiting for help to arrive, and I was trying to tell her how much I loved her, while stroking her hair and face. I was trying to wake her up and had a wash cloth wiping her face to clean off the drool. They finally came into the house and they asked me to move aside. They were working fast and furiously and I was watching everything. One of them asked me where my Dad was and I told them that Lee was my Step Dad and that he was back in the bedroom and didn't want to help her and that he was drunk anyway. I saw him come out of his room and look down the hall towards us and he yelled out, "Let her die!" The medics didn't even seem to be phased by his comment and they kept right on working. Lee went to the bathroom and went back to his room.

Aunt Faye and Uncle George got there as the ambulance was leaving and they were able to tell them to which hospital she should go. Aunt Faye told me that she couldn't take me to sit up at the hospital with them all night, but that she would come back that next morning and pick me up and take me to the hospital to see her. She told me to go and pray for Mother and told me that everything would be OK. She wanted me to go to sleep. It was very late at night by now.

When the ambulance left, the phone rang and it was Terry. She just wanted to know if I was OK and what had happened. I told her all about it and Lee stepped into the room. He sounded gruff and told me to get off the phone and that I wasn't to get calls that late at night. It was sometime around midnight and I usually didn't get calls that late, but Terry was worried. She could see our house from her bedroom window just 5 lots away. The lots between us were vacant, so she had a clear view. Anyway, I did as I was told, even though I didn't like this guy one bit!!! He was a loser in my eyes, just like Mother said! Anyone who wouldn't help out someone dying was scum!

I lay in my bed for a while listening and waiting for Lee to go to sleep. I couldn't hear anything moving after about 20 minutes, and I was afraid that I might accidentally fall asleep before he did and before I had heard any news from Aunt Faye. Aunt Faye had warned me that it would probably take a while for them to find out anything. I decided to get up and go to the bathroom and then wet my face to keep me awake. While I was in the bathroom, I heard the doorknob jiggle. I told Lee that I was in there and that I would be out in just a minute. He walked back to his room without a comment.

I went on back to my room and was lying on my bed and Lee walked in. Dang! What was he doing walking in my room? He came and sat down on my bed beside me and asked me to lay back down. He started rubbing my shoulder and telling me that he was sorry that he didn't help. He was telling me that he really did love my mother but that he just couldn't do anything right and all kinds of other stuff. I wasn't very comfortable with him rubbing on my arm like that. I didn't trust him at all! He asked me if I would forgive him and of course I would say yes, and then he asked me if I loved him. Well, he was so drunk that I thought that the right answer at this point would be to say, "YES" so that's what I said. He finally got up and said that he was going to bed and that he would go see Mother in the morning.

Lee finally went to sleep around 3:00am and I was able to make sure that he didn't have a cigarette lit and I went to bed. I said my prayers and asked God one more time to take care of Mother and eventually fell asleep.

I woke up fairly late the next morning and found that Lee was gone. It was Saturday, thank goodness, so I hadn't missed anything. I called Aunt Faye's house, but there was no answer and I had no idea how to call her at the hospital so I had to wait for her call. At about 10:00am Aunt Faye called and said that she and Uncle George were on their way to pick me up to go see Mother.

I got dressed and ready to go and I told them that I didn't know where Lee was. They told me that they saw him at the hospital that morning and left when he had arrived so that he and Mother could talk if they let him in.

We headed to the hospital and I asked them how Mother was? They said that the emergency room people had pumped her stomach and were able to save her but that she had taken a very dangerous drug and they made her stay the night in the ER to make sure she was going to be alright. When she was stable, they took her up to a room and they got to talk to her for a minute. They told me that she wasn't in a very good mood when they saw her but maybe Lee could do something. I told them how Lee was just going to let her die, that he had been drinking a lot and they just told me that if Mother loved him enough to marry him, then Mother and Lee would have to work that out.

We arrived at the hospital and I was so eager to see Mother. I just knew that she would be so happy to see me and I was so proud of myself for saving her life! We stepped off the elevator onto her floor and soon as we stepped off the elevator, I could see her down the hall, sitting up in the bed arguing with someone that she didn't need any of their help. I walked into the room and before, I could say hello, she turned and glared at me and yelled out, "And you! I hate you!!! Why did you call for help? I wanted to die!!! I told you to let me die!!! If I wanted your help I would have asked you, but I told you that I wanted to die!!! Why couldn't you let me die like I asked???" Aunt Faye spoke up and told her that she shouldn't be blaming me for trying to help and Aunt Faye took me out of the room and took me home. She told me how sorry she was that Mother had yelled those terrible things to me and how sad she was that Mother never did treat me right. She dropped me off at home and said that she would go back to the hospital to see if she could get things straightened out and that she would call me later and let me know what was going on.

To my surprise, Aunt Faye, Uncle George and Lee had brought Mother home that afternoon and Aunt Faye kept going back and forth into her bedroom to talk to her about admitting herself to an institution for help. Mother went into the kitchen and she still had that angry look about her. She was pouring herself a drink, this time a large one (straight from the bottle)! She told everyone to just leave her alone, she didn't want any help from anyone! Aunt Faye mentioned something to her about not needing that drink and Mother went and grabbed the gallon jug and took it to her room and told them that she did need it and that was ALL she needed!

Aunt Faye and Uncle George left and said that there was nothing that they could do for her if she didn't want to help herself. Aunt Faye looked at me and told me that she was sorry but that she had tried.

Mother stayed in her room all day and never came out except for the bathroom.

She and Lee argued that night, but they ended early this night. I was able to go to sleep before midnight this time.

Mother called Aunt Faye the next day and asked her to come over and talk to her.

Aunt Faye and Uncle George came over again and they went into the bedroom to talk. Mother was telling them that she decided that she did want to place herself into Big Springs Hospital on a voluntary basis for help. Mother told her that I was suppose to go to my Daddy's house for Christmas in two days and so he would be able to take care of me while she was gone. Aunt Faye made arrangements for her and the next day, Lee and I were to drive her there.

It seemed like a very long drive, but it was only an hour or two. When we drove up at the hospital, I got kind of scared. Aunt Faye said that it was a mental institution and the only thing that I knew about these places was what I had seen on the movies. I had seen them do shock treatments on patients and I was worried that they would do the same to her. We walked up the steps and in through the big double doors. The nurses were all wearing all white nurses' dresses, like Mother wore when she worked. Some one came up and met Mother near the entry and told her to tell us good-bye and she would take her to settle in. I asked the lady right then if they did shock therapy at this place and Mother was embarrassed that I had asked that. The lady laughed and told me that they wouldn't do anything like that to Mother and that they were just going to help her.

Well, it was clear that it was time for Lee and me to go and so we got back into the car and drove all the way back home. Since it was December by now, the nights came early and we drove back beginning at sundown. We got home in time to see if there was anything on the television. We sat in the living room and watched TV and Lee poured himself a drink and watched too. While watching TV, I told Lee that my back was sore from the long drive. Lee told me that it was probably because I was laying on the floor watching TV. I asked him if he would pop my back like my Daddy does and he said that he would try. He came and strattled my back and I told him how to place his hands so that he wouldn't hurt my spine and he tried a few times to pop it. Then, he started rubbing something else on my bottom! He was rubbing his private back and forth across my bottom!!! His pants were on, but I figured out real fast what was going on. I jumped up and went to my room. He asked me where I was going and I didn't want any conflicts, so I just told him that I needed to go pack and get to bed early since Daddy was coming in the morning. He never knew that I figured out what he was doing.

The next morning was great! I was going to be with my daddy!

Daddy arrived by noon and we headed to Waco. I was on top of the world! He said that we would have to stop by Aunt Sue's first and pick up Bud. Bud stayed there at their house Monday through Friday while Dad drove the truck so that someone could take care of him. He had it made cause Aunt Sue was really nice and he got along great with Larry - my youngest cousin. Aunt Sue was my Daddy's stepsister and she was married to Uncle Red. Now he was scary! He had a very gruff voice and when he spoke, we listened. They had five kids. Dennis was the oldest and he was a teenager by now and so was his younger brother Tim. Larry was about 10 or 11 years old and they all shared the same room together and Bud did too during the week. Cindy was about 13 years old and Susan was my age - 12. The most noticeable thing about this family was that they were all Red-Heads except for Aunt Sue and Tim with their dark brown, almost black hair! They all had freckles too! I asked Daddy if we could stay and visit so that I could visit Susan a little while and so he agreed. Susan and I were favorite cousins! We could talk about everything!!! This always made Cindy mad because we didn't tell her anything. Susan said that she told her mother everything and so we kept to ourselves and would rarely let Cindy get involved.

I spent the next few hours filling Susan in on all that had gone on since the last time we saw each other. It had been a long time. Since the rest of Daddy's family shunned him for taking Uncle D to court, we hadn't seen each other at all. Susan told me that her Momma believed me about Uncle D and that she just didn't think that they wanted to admit that it was true, because it would hurt them more to know the truth. It was easier to deny it. Well, that was comforting to hear. At least somebody believed me. They didn't tell their opinions to the rest of the family though; they said that they didn't think that it would do any good.

Well, our visit was over soon and Daddy rounded us up and promised me that we would see them again before I went back home. Daddy had to go to work the next day but would be home that evening. He was on some special run during Christmas holidays so that he could spend time with us. He made us promise that we would stay out of trouble while he worked during the day and we both assured him that everything would be fine.

Bud and I got along great during the day while Daddy was at work. He took me to the creek and we went craw fishing. This was a smelly adventure. That nearly dry creek had lots of mosquitoes and was stagnant. Bud was good at this stuff! He actually caught one! He threw it back in after he showed me. Oh, it stunk! Yuck!

He showed me around everywhere. He had a couple a neighbor friends that we played with all day until Daddy got home.

Daddy came home and we ate dinner and then he went into the bedroom and was on the telephone for a long time. I eventually went in to see when he was going to be off the phone. He had talked for over an hour. I could tell by the smile on his face and the gleam in his eye that he had to be talking to a lady. He told me to go on so I went back in to watch TV with Bud. Thirty minutes later, he came out and sat down. I just had to ask who he was talking to and asked him to tell me all about her!!

He was glowing. He told us that he had been talking to this really nice lady on the phone for a few days and that he was really wanting to meet her. I was so happy for him. He told us that he was going to meet her on Friday night - only two days away. He asked me if I knew anything about hair color and I told him that I knew a little so he asked me if I would help him out. He didn't want this new lady to think that he was an old man or something. We found the "Grecian formula 44 for Men" and started to work. In just 30 minutes, we had a slightly younger looking Daddy! I told him that he wouldn't have a thing to worry about anyway, because he was the perfect man that any woman would be lucky to have. He just smiled and said that he hoped so.

It was really cute seeing my Daddy primping and making a big fuss about meeting a lady. The big night was here and she was coming here to meet him so that they wouldn't get such a late start. She lived in Fort Worth, an hour and a half drive away. If he left to drive up there, after coming home from work, then he wouldn't get there until at least 7:00pm and so she had agreed that they would like to make the most of their time, so she would make the drive down. He took care of paying for her gas though. My Daddy was always a perfect gentleman!

Well, the moment which we had all been waiting for had arrived. Daddy yelled from his room, "She's here!" He ran in and told Bud and I to turn off the TV for a while until they left on their date. He asked us to be really nice to her. Of course we would. We wouldn't make him look bad at all.

She came in wearing a red and white polka dotted dress with a wide white Patton leather belt. She was kind of short, had very dark hair and was very pretty. Her name was Bee (not her true name). I felt uncomfortable to call her Bee, but I quickly introduced myself and started talking her ears off. She asked us what we had been doing that day, and I spoke up and told her that Bud's friends were teaching us how to pass out. It was really fun and Bud and I would demonstrate it for her if she would like! She asked me what I meant by "passing out" and I told her that you can hold your breath and another person squeezes you real tight and you just pass out! She declined the demo but was very polite about it saying that this was probably not a very safe thing to be doing. I just smiled at her ignorance. It was fun! You just had to do it first to see, but of course I didn't bother her any further details because Daddy was looking at me funny. I had just highly embarrassed him with my little story. He made the right move by suggesting that they get on their way before they were late to their dinner reservations.

They were out very late and I watched my Daddy kiss her good-bye as he helped her into her car.

Daddy walked in yelling "Oh Boy!" We asked him how he liked her and he said that this was only their first date, but so far, she was great!

She had invited Daddy to bring us up the next day to spend the evening at her house. We drove up to her house and arrived at about 6:00pm and saw her beautiful two-story home with Christmas lights on it. She met us at the door smiling and welcomed us all in. She spoke to Bud and me, so that we wouldn't feel left out and then introduced us to her dog "Poppy". He was a beautiful Dalmatian. She told us about his prize pedigree and all that, but I wasn't really too sure how important that was. All I could tell was that he was beautiful and friendly.

She had prepared some dessert for us for after dinner. It was apple pie! She surely was a good cook! That was one of Daddy's favorites too! Bud and I sat and watched TV that evening in the den after dessert, while she and Daddy talked in the living room. I decided to go see how things were going and I went in and saw her sitting holding Daddy's hand. Wow! Things must be going pretty good! I talked to them for a little while and we asked questions back and forth and I saw her pretty watch that she was wearing. I went over and sat in between her and Daddy and asked her if I could see it. She took it off her arm and gave it to me. I told her that I just wanted to look at it and then she insisted that I keep it. Wow! I couldn't believe that she just gave me the watch off her own arm. What a nice lady!!!

I went back in the den to check out my new treasure and to finish watching the movie. Bud and I had watched a whole movie and it was now 10:00pm. I went back into the living room and to my surprise, she was sitting on his lap and they were smooching!!! I went back into the den and thought that it would be best to call out Daddy's name before I walked back in so they would have warning. When I returned, they were finished kissing but she was still in his lap. He told me that we would leave in another 30 minutes and asked me to go back and watch a little more TV until we left. I understood!

Well, Daddy talked about her most of the way home. He just kept on saying what a sweet lady she was and I was in full agreement. Bud didn't say much but did agree that she seemed nice.

During the week, I found Daddy on the phone in the evenings just like a teenager. It was kind of cute to see him all lit up. They were making plans for the following weekend.

She, Daddy, Bud and I spent almost the entire weekend together.

One evening after she had gone home, I told Daddy that he was on to something really special. He agreed. I told him that he shouldn't waste any-more time and that he should ask her to marry him. He turned and asked, "You really think so?" I told him that she was definitely the right person. He, to my surprise, had told me that he had been thinking about doing that. He said that he knew it was kind of early, but was sure and wanted to get on with things and that he just might do that.

A few days later, he announced to us that he had popped the question. He told us that they were getting married. I asked him when, and he said that they were ready to this weekend! What!!!!!!! I had to ask again for confirmation! My ears had not deceived me. I asked him where they were going to marry and he told me that it was a church in Waco. I asked which one and he told me it was a Seventh day Adventist Church. A what? I had never heard of one of those. I was raised a Baptist, had visited the Church of Christ but never heard of a Seventh Day something. I asked him what they do and he said that they were kind of like the Baptist Church except they go to church on Saturday. He said that he was going to go to a few Bible studies with her to find out more about it since that's what she was.

Well, I trusted my Dad that he wouldn't get into the wrong thing and before I knew it, it was their wedding day. He was baptized right before the wedding because she had told him that she didn't want to marry outside of her church. He accepted the seventh day Sabbath and had no problem with becoming a member.

Daddy had called the few family members, that still cared about us after the Uncle D ordeal, and invited them to the wedding. Granddaddy B and Granny E were there along with Aunt Sue and her family. The wedding was very short and simple.

Bud and I spent the weekend at Aunt Sue's house while they went on their honeymoon. The honeymoon had to be brief for now because Daddy had to take me back to Abilene in just a few days. I regretted that!

Time was up and it was time to return to the hell zone. When Daddy dropped me off at the door and kissed me good-bye, I walked into the house and to my surprise, Mother was there! I (in a state of astonishment) asked, "What are you doing here?!!!" She meanly said, "I live here, what do mean what am I doing here?" I replied to her that I just meant that I thought that she was still at the hospital and she told me that she didn't like that place and came home. I quickly noticed that She and Lee had drinks in their hands and so I was prepared for the battles ahead.

They started quickly! That very next night! The fights weren't too bad at first but they progressively got worse. After a couple of weeks, they were right back like they used to be, to the point where I was losing sleep night after night.

By March, I had taken all I could stand. I went to school one morning and made a collect call to my Daddy. I didn't know if he would be there or not and when the operator announced a collect call from me, Bee accepted and told me that he would be home on Friday and she told me to call back then.

Friday seemed to come so slowly and I worried all week wondering what he would say to my question.

Finally, it was Friday. I told my teacher that I would be late to class because I needed to call my Daddy and she gave me permission. I dialed collect from the pay phone there and he accepted the call. He asked me why I was calling and I told him that things were really bad at home and I was wondering if they would let me come and live with them? He told me that this was a really big question. I knew it was. He had just gotten married and all. He said that he would first have to talk to her about it and if she agreed, then I would have to get Mother to agree to sign over custody. He didn't think that Mother would do that since she would loose the child support. He told me to get to a phone on Sunday and call him back and he would let me know what Bee's decision was.

Sunday was finally here. I had worried all weekend about her deciding to take on a new kid. Surely she would though because we had really hit it off before they married! Well, I got a big piece of GOOD NEWS!!! She said that we could try it out BUT I had to get the second part of the plan accomplished. I had to get Mother to sign over custody.

I went home and decided to pray about the matter first. Then, I had to find the right opportunity to talk to Mother. I didn't want to hurt her feelings or anything so I decided to approach her with the fact that I was in their way, and that She and Lee would probably get along better without me and she didn't get mad at me for asking. She didn't look happy either, but she hadn't looked happy since her suicide attempt. She told me that she would think about it and tell me later.

Well, that wasn't a no!

A few days later, when she was mad at Lee about something, she came and looked at me and yelled, "You can get the hell out of here too!" I asked her what she meant and she sarcastically reminded me of my question to her. I asked her if she meant that she would sign over custody and she said that she would gladly get rid of me!

Well, that's not how I was wanting to get the news but I would take it however it came.

I asked her if I could call Daddy collect and she said that she didn't care what I did. So, I made the call. He wasn't home, so I talked to Bee. She told me that she would try to get word to him about all this and she asked me to call her back the next day and she would let me know what he said about when they could come and get me.

By Friday, I was gone. Daddy and Bee both came to pick me up, but Bee stayed in the car. I had all my stuff packed and Daddy had to go and make sure with Mother that she was certain about letting me live with him. He asked her to put it into writing so that he wouldn't have any problems with the courts and she jotted a quick note down and very simply stated, "I, Marcia, give all custody of Cathy to her dad, Bill." She signed it and dated it and we were off! My new life had just begun! Now I would be with my Daddy and have a mother that would love me too. I couldn't have asked for anything any better.

Chapter 5: The whole new life!

The drive to Fort Worth didn't seem very long because I had so much to think about. Bud was already living there and I wondered how we would get along. Since Mother wasn't there to baby him all the time, then maybe things would be better for us. I wondered where my room would be. I didn't even know if her two sons lived there. Bee had a teenage son named Stan (not his true name) and he was going to graduate this year from high school and she mentioned an older son named Bob (not his true name). She had said that he was going to college. I wondered where Bud's room was. And where would I go to school? Would this would be a big change from Lincoln Jr. High? I also was thinking about her Saturday church.

My day dream soon stopped when Bee handed me a tissue and asked me to wipe off my makeup. I looked at her oddly wondering whatever was wrong with my makeup. I wasn't wearing very much so I asked her, "What makeup?" She said, "All that blue or black stuff around your eyes." Oh! She must be speaking of my navy blue eye liner. I wore that all the time. "It's in style," I replied. She told me that she thought that I was too young and didn't need that stuff and that it made me look cheap. I never heard anyone say anything bad about my makeup before, but I didn't want to do anything to upset her, so I quickly worked at getting it off. She thanked me and told me that I looked much better without it.

After daydreaming for a while longer, I saw a sign that read, "FT. WORTH". I asked Daddy if we were there and he said that we were near, so I started looking around at my new surroundings. This city is definitely prettier than Abilene because there are trees and hills instead of flat land and sand.

We walked in and Bee directed me toward my new room. She told me that this had been the guest room, but right now that was the only spare room. Well, I was more than happy to stay in there because it was beautiful. It was decorated in pink and had an old fashioned dressing table, a queen size bed and it was just perfect. I began unpacking my things and she made me feel at home by cleaning her things out of the closet and some of the drawers. She ran in and cooked dinner while I finished up.

By bedtime, I was able to lie down in my bed without fear of any drunken brawls. Peace and quiet.!!

Bud and I were having fun getting reacquainted. There was lots of news to catch up on. He was a little bit surprised to hear about Mother's suicide attempt and angry that her husband was a louse to push her to that point. At least he felt that it was his fault. Mother never seemed to be happy though, no matter which husband she had. I asked Bud how the new school was and he said it was OK. What type of response should I have expected from someone who could care less about school though?

Bee had to take me to get me checked in at my new school on Monday. It was Wedgwood Middle School and it was nice. Bee usually drove us to school every morning and we had to walk home. It was only a mile away. Believe me, we would have rather walked to school too, than to have her drive us up there with her housecoat and hair thing on. She wore this ugly blue satiny thing that was a net on top. It was supposed to keep her hair from messing up while she slept. For a teen, it is NOT cool to be seen with someone wearing that. We would ask her to drop us off way down the block so no one would see us get out of the car. We would just die if we were seen, especially since I was new. To top it off, the ultimate embarrassment - she would stop at the gas station at least two or three times a week to buy $.50 worth of gas and if she felt rich that day, she added a $1.00. Thank goodness, she didn't have to get out of the car to fill it up. I mean, I felt sorry for the attendant having to go to that trouble for such a small sale, but it was far better than her getting out. She thought that it was really funny that the attendant knew her so well that they hand signals worked out between them to show $1 or $.50.

I made friends very quickly with our neighbors on each side of us.

Mitzi and Toby B. lived on our left. Toby was my age, had dark brown hair and wore glasses. He later became my boyfriend. Mitzi was a year younger. She reminded me of Mary Ann on Gilligan's Island, because of how she looked and did her hair. She and Bud were an item for a very short time. I guess they thought that it would be nice to try for convenience sake. Their house had a play room in the back, which had a pool table and a stereo, and this was a perfect spot for us to hang out if it were too hot or cold outside.

Karla and her little sister lived next door on the right. Karla had long, straight, blonde hair and was kind of tall and thin like I was. Karla's dad was a Lutheran Minister and her mom stayed at home to raise the family.

The three of us girls were close enough in age to have a great time together. As soon as Bud and I were finished with homework. (I rarely I had homework to do because I did my work in class and Bud would never admit to having any even if he were failing) The chores had to be finished as well, then, we would be gone to hang out with them until our curfew time. Depending on which season it was, we usually came in when the street lights came on and we would know to help get dinner on the table. Bee cooked and we set the table. She had this thing about setting the table with every tool and accessory for every meal! What a waste of perfectly clean dishes. I wanted to teach her how to economize, but I could tell that this tradition was in stone!

After I was there for about two weeks, Daddy came in to my room and asked me if he could ask me a big favor. My Daddy rarely started off a conversation like this, so I was all ears. He said that Bee really didn't like being called Bee and she would really like it if I would call her Mom and he would really appreciate it too. He explained to me that she was being a Mom to me, so it shouldn't seem unrealistic to call her that. I didn't have a problem with calling her Mom, in fact, I felt kind of honored that she wanted me to call her Mom. It made me feel like she was trying to be a real mother to me. (Just like the Mother that I had always dreamed of having.) I didn't like calling her by her first name anyway because I was raised to feel that this was a sign of disrespect.

I decided to mention to Daddy that I would like to begin calling him Dad now instead of Daddy, because it just seemed like a more grown-up word. He said that he didn't mind.

Bee taught Piano, Voice and Flute lessons and so most afternoons, we had to be very quiet inside the house because she taught in the living room and it was very easy to disturb her. That is why she didn't mind us going outside after we came in from school. Even the TV bothered her.

After I had lived there for 3 months, I really learned how bothered she could be when teaching her lessons. I was in the kitchen on the telephone talking to Karla to make arrangements to meet outside when she was finished with her work and while we were talking, Stan picked up the phone upstairs and began dialing a number (without listening first to see if it was in use). I spoke up to tell Stan that I was on the phone and he yelled at me to get off. I was trying to talk quietly so that I wouldn't disturb the music lesson in the next room and so I told him that I would be off in a few minutes. He yelled at me to get off now! Then he started pushing the dialing buttons so that they would squeal in my ear and then Karla and I couldn't talk at all. I tried to get a word in to him to tell him that if he would hang up, then I would tell her good-bye and he could have the phone, but he kept butting in. Now, when you are on a telephone extension, and someone picks up another and begins talking, the voice from your extension is much louder than from the other party being called. I was trying really had to keep the squealing phone quiet, but Stan persisted and I obviously bothered Mom.

Mom came around the corner and asked me angrily, "What is all that noise? Can't you keep it quiet in here while I'm teaching?" I began trying to explain that it was Stan upstairs trying to be rude and he wouldn't let me say good-bye to Karla and she told me that she wanted me to hang up and be quiet. I again tried to explain that I wasn't making the noise and then she turned and walked into her room in a huff and I tried to tell Stan that he was making too much noise and he was still holding down the buttons making the phone squeal. Upon her immediate return, she came in with a belt!!! I was very surprised and I thought that she was going up to yell at Stan, but instead, she was coming at me. I hung up the phone and she swung it at me, hitting me across the leg! I took a step forward and tried to explain to her again and she swung again and hit me across the back. Then I ran to the stairs and fell at the turn of the third step and she just kept swinging the belt in a rage!!! I was curled up in a ball to try to protect my face and the front part of my body from the strapping! She had hit me about seven or eight times before she stopped swinging. She was screaming, saying that the only thing that she asks of us was to be quiet while she taught, and her facing that embarrass-ment, and that their parents were paying money for these lessons, and how she might lose her students because of these interruptions, and on, and on, and on!!!

I cried as I faced the reality that I had moved from one hell hole to another. At least, Mother had quit beating me by this time. Now, I'm right back in the same mess. I just couldn't believe how she lost it over something so petty. If she had have asked me nicely to hang up, listened to my quick explanation and then told me that she still wanted me to hang up, then I would have done so immediately. I may not have liked her decision, but it wouldn't have been any big deal. My disgust was with Stan! Had he given me one moment, then

I would have surrendered the phone.

I never told Dad about the ordeal because I was too scared. Remember, he was gone Sunday night through Friday morning, and I would have to be with her all week. I lost respect for her quickly over that ordeal. I thought that she was very unfair! I would have understood if I were the one to blame, but she didn't even care about who's fault it was! Bud overheard the whole thing and came and got me from the stairs and told me that she yells at him all the time like that. He told me right then, that he didn't like her because she was a nag and that he didn't like her hitting me that way. He told me that Stan always gets his way about everything.

I found some clothes to cover up my wounds and later went out to talk with the girls. Karla asked me why she had started yelling at me and when I explained it to them, they asked if I was alright. I showed them the marks all over my back and legs. They were shocked. They said that their parents never did that to them. They said that they had been spanked, but only on the behind.

Thank goodness that I didn't hold grudges. I forgave her soon, and just always remembered to keep quiet during her lessons.

We went to her church as she had asked. I tried to ask Dad if I could ride the Church Bus to go to the Baptist Church instead of her church, but Dad didn't like that idea. He wanted our family to go together and so did she. I went and made friends there, but it wasn't easy. When kids would ask me who my parents were, I would tell them that my Dad had married Bee and when they couldn't figure out who I was speaking of, I would tell them her former name - Bee Wolsley. "OH!" They obviously knew that name! Sometimes they would laugh or begin whispering. I didn't know what they were so shocked about but a few of the girls informed me that she was the meanest lady in the whole church. "How did they know," I wondered? They had heard rumors from the older kids at church about her from things that Bob and Stan used to tell. Their parents knew of her reputation as well. I defended her and told them that she was pretty nice until that episode happened on the stairs and then I knew what they meant!

Summer came quickly and she wanted to send us to church camp. Mom told Dad that we would have a lot of fun there and that it would be nice for them to go on a vacation while we were there, especially since they had not had a real honeymoon. She told us that it costs a lot but that they had fun things to do and that it lasts for a whole week and that there would be lots of kids our age there. I asked some of the kids at church if they were going and there was one girl that wanted to go and Mom and Dad agreed to give her a ride. Well, this sounded OK. I had been to a Church Camp years ago from the Baptist Church and it was lots of fun.

It took a few hours to drive there. The name of it was "Lone Star Camp" and it was in Athens, TX. It was just on the edge of where the pine and cedar trees began. There were several cabins throughout the area and a large covered eating area. It was built around a small lake. We got registered and then found out our assigned cabins. Mom and Dad helped us to unload and they were off. I quickly got my things organized so that I could go check out the surroundings. We only had a short time before we would have to be at our first gathering. Wow! What a place. She was right! There were lots of things to do. I signed up for Swimming, Skiing, and Plaster crafts.

In order to take swimming class, you had to test your skill level so that they would know in which class to place you. I was told to take Intermediate and I would have to wait until the next year to water ski because I had to have an Intermediate level in order to ski. I changed the schedule to include Leather crafts since skiing was out.

The week went by so fast. I had met lots of kids and some cute guys too. I passed my Intermediate Swimming class so this meant that I could ski next year. I regretted having to go home and miss all of my new friends. This was the most fun that I had ever had in my entire life. I couldn't wait 'till next year.

When they picked us up, I gave Mom a big hug for thinking about this. I gave Dad one too because I knew that it wasn't cheap and it was a long drive. They told us that they had a fun time too, while they had been gone!

The next surprise that she had in mind had me a little bit more nervous. She told Dad that she would like for Bud and I to go to the church school for 8th grade. What church school and WHY? She told us about it and that it was an Adventist school and that it would be better for us to get a Christian Education than going to Public Schools. The cost of this was really high too. I was just fine with continuing where I was. I had experienced enough changes for a while. She insisted though telling my dad that she felt this was best, so he went along with her advice.

Bud and I went to visit for registration. We were NOT impressed. It was "rinky-dink"! The classrooms were small and had two grades in the same class. We would be in a 7th - 8th grade class. OH BOY! I always wanted to be in 7th grade again! (Actually, I really resented the idea!) There wasn't even a gym. All sports had to be played outside and what about if it rained? What was she getting us into. Another bad point - sack lunches!*#@^*# Barf! It was bad enough that we had to eat veggie-meat at home but now we would have to pack it in a lunch!

Oh! I guess I forgot to tell you that she was vegetarian, so we had to be also. Some of the food was OK but some was rank! She was a good cook for what she had to cook with, but I missed my Chicken and Hamburgers. Instead, we had fried Soy-Chick and Veggie-Burgers. The Veggie-Burgers weren't too bad if they were done right. Some people were so good at this stuff that you could hardly tell that they weren't real! Her best dish was Spaghetti. Everyone in the church liked it. She always took that to Pot Luck. Pot Luck is a meal where everyone at church brings a dish and they all share it after the service is over, for lunch. Sometimes those meals were interesting. Sometimes there were some great dishes and some that looked good but WEREN'T!

Back to school! Our convincing argument against this new school didn't work, so, when the first day of school opened, we went to that school. The name of the school was Burton Jr. Academy. It was called a Jr. Academy because it only went through the 10th grade. It was obvious that I would be attending here for 3 long years. The first new venture was that we had to catch the bus. The Burton bus picked up students all over the Ft. Worth Metroplex and therefore; you do not get front door service. They stopped at a bank parking lot along the highway about 3/4 miles from home. It wasn't too bad except when the bus was late. By the way! She still wore that goofy robe, slippers and hair thing. We were so embarrassed! Especially when she got out and talked to some of the other mothers at the bus stop. She knew them all. One day, as we were in a hurry to make it on time, she didn't have time to stop and get her $.50 worth of gas and so the car died of starvation and we had to walk to the gas station with her in the goofy getup! Does she not think about these things beforehand? In the afternoons, the bus let us out at the same spot and we had to walk home because she would be teaching music lessons.

There was one bonus about this new school! The kids from the church went there too. Before long, I had made good friends with Pam and Liz , Melanie, and Dante and Robert. Robert and Pam were in the 7th grade, Liz was in the 6th, and the rest of us were in 8th. We all went to the same Ft. Worth Church together. Two other girls from the church went, Rhonda and Schantile . Rhonda was in the 7th grade but her sister was in the 6th. They went to our church too. There were several others from our church that attended that were brothers and sisters of these, or in different grade levels. The pastor's daughter Deanne and her sister went too. Bud's friend from church, who was a year or two older, named Mike, went as well. So, it wasn't as though we were going to be total strangers here.

Our teacher was very nice and very pretty. Her name was Miss Miller. She was single. She taught English and history and a few other classes. We had the same subjects as in any other school except we had Bible class each day. We also had gymnastics classes. This school was quite inventive on new ways to have fun. We raised money to buy a foosball table and an air hockey table and later, we even got a trampoline. That's the one I liked. I stayed at the trampoline every day that it was set up. We could use it indoors or outdoors. There was a large auditorium that we could use when the weather was bad. The Principal was a really nice man. Of course, in all schools you have the snobs.

My brother gained popularity by his usual method. If he could publicly insult and embarrass his sister in front of everyone, then people would think he was funny. If he made them laugh, then he could gain friends. He didn't care at all, that it was at my expense! He went to school and started telling the other kids that my dog liked me (and I'm not talking like in a normal "man to man's best friend" relationship either). What he was talking about was sick and disgusting, but everyone thought it was funny and so they laughed at me and started calling me "Woofy" and "Brandog"! I would walk down the hall and others would just start barking at me or calling me as though they would their dog! I was SO humiliated! The stupid name calling stuck for the entire year! I could have killed him. I was already having enough problems at school when the kids found out that I was the daughter of Bee Wolsley. I tried to correct them to understand that I was only the STEP daughter but it didn't help any. Her reputation was known throughout the Seventh-day Adventist realm! To top it off, she took me to a store before school started and bought me a bunch of "old lady pantsuits". The were double knit hounds-tooth pattern and she swore to me that all the kids in private school wore those kinds of clothes. She said that the school rules were that no girls could wear dresses where the hem was above the knee or any pants where the top didn't cover the hips. (This was called tunic-length.) She assured me that these rules were strictly enforced and that there were absolutely NO JEANS ALLOWED! Well, those rules were written in the handbook, but I was probably the ONLY student who was adhering to the rules. Everyone else wore jeans and dresses that were 3 - 4 inches above the knee but she told me that no daughter of hers would be seen in men's style pants. I asked her what she meant by that and she said that any pants that zipped up the front were men's style and that this was a sin for a woman to dress like an man. I wasn't trying to dress like a man! I just wanted to wear what other girls were wearing! They always made fun of my stupid clothes.

I faced so much continual ridicule during my 8th grade year, that I wanted to die. I really couldn't take anymore. I had very few friends at my own grade level because it was not cool to be seen with a dog. Even my few friends that I did have, would occasionally join in the teasing! They would apologize to me later, but that was after the others had left and they wouldn't look bad in front of them. There was only one other by in the school to get this much ridicule. They teased him because he was overweight and he was so attention starved, that he acted obnoxious. He was over at our house all the time and we got along pretty well there, but around others, he would do some real stupid things for attention. I was guilty of joining in teasing him and he also joined in with the others in teasing me. There always has to be someone that everyone teases and we were the targets there.

Eighth grade was the very worst year of my life! My social life at school was terrible! This caused my church life to be horrible also since the same kids went there, and my home life was a wreck living with Mom! That first beating she gave me wasn't the last and it seemed as though she had a guide to go by to cause her daughter to become the least popular in school. I mean, she actually thought that it would be cute to make me a "Calypso" outfit. I didn't know what it was until she had finished it on the sewing machine. The top had three different solid colors and one pattern of flowers that she did in block sections and then made the puff sleeves the same way. She finished it off by adding extra wide yellow/gold Rick Rack around the edges of the pants, sleeves and bottom of the "tunic-length" top. I called it my "CLOWN SUIT!" All I needed was a big, red nose and bright, red curly wig and I would be able to join the Circus! The other kids thought so too. The first day I wore it, I was teased unmercifully!

She later made some other clothes that were at least not as bad as this, but they certainly weren't anything that any other girls asked to borrow!

Before I knew it, eighth grade had come to a close. The ending of eighth grade at Burton was a big celebration. They had a real "Cap & Gown" ceremonial graduation and everything! There was a big swimming party planned afterwards at one of the student's home. It was even fun making the plans for it.

The caps and gowns arrived at school toward the end of the year and since they were stored in boxes, we were told that they would need to be ironed first. A classmate, Melody, said that she needed someone to iron hers because she didn't have an iron, so I volunteered to help her. Bud liked her so I figured that this was a way to make two people happy.

When the day came, Bud came and asked me to iron his gown too. He wasn't very good at doing such things and this was a chance for me to have him be doubly nice to me. I was going to iron his gown and his girlfriend's. He might be nice to me the whole day for this! I enjoyed ironing and fell into daydreaming about a real high school graduation while doing it. Suddenly, I looked at my watch and realized that I needed to get busy because I also needed to pack extra clothes and a swimsuit and towel for the party afterward. I wasn't even dressed yet.

I had everything accomplished and on time and Bud and I were just waiting for Mom to finish her last music lesson so we could go. We were always late, everywhere we went! She just couldn't get everything done that she had scheduled. She crammed her schedule too tight and this always made her run late. I had my hair done, three gowns ironed, three caps, swimsuit and towel, clothes, and was dressed in the new dress Mom had made for me. It was bright pink and was even kind of pretty for a double knit dress.

Finally, she called for us! We came running the stairs with everything we needed. We might make it on time, for once! We loaded into the car and headed to the Arlington church, where the graduation would be. As we were driving there, Mom spoke up and asked me if I got the nuts. "What nuts", I asked. In her normal panic stricken voice, she told me that they were on the kitchen table. I told her that she hadn't told me about any nuts or I would have packed them. Suddenly, she slammed on the brakes and screamed at me that she was supposed to bring nuts to the reception and she told me to pack everything for this graduation and during this railing, she doubled up her fist and back-handed me right in the mouth! (Now realize that we are on the highway going about 70 mph in a 55 mph zone and when she slammed on the brakes, we were only going about 5 mph and facing certain traffic hazards - LIKE BEING REAR-ENDED BY ANOTHER VEHICLE GO-ING 55mph!!!) After being hit in the mouth and nose with this single blow, I grabbed my face! Just in time - to catch the flow of blood coming from my nose and busted lip! Then I started crying. How could she blame me for her mistakes?!!! I had been very responsible to get everything ready and had she just told me about her responsibility, I would have done it too. Bud pipes up and says, "Wow, way to go Mom! That's just great! I guess she's going to get blood everywhere!" Boy he was mad at her. I had never heard him speak up to her like that and especially taking up for me! He quickly grabbed some Kleenex and handed them to me to catch the blood before it got on my new dress. Bee told him to shut up and not to butt in anymore. She then started telling us how the other mothers, who were planning the reception for us, had called her and asked her to bring something and she felt relieved when they had just asked her to bring a can of mixed nuts because she knew that she was going to be busy, and how she would look like a fool for not even doing this simple request. She was worried that she was going to look bad,. AGAIN! She didn't even say that she was sorry for busting my lip and didn't even ask how I was. She just drove off in a rush, like a bat out of Hades, to try to get back on schedule. She was still going on and on about how we always make her look bad.

When we arrived, I got out of the car in a fury! I grabbed my purse and ran to the restroom, but before I could get there to see how bad I looked, I caught a glimpse of Pam and Melanie and they saw my face and hurried with me to the bathroom to see what had happened. I couldn't believe my eyes! I looked even worse than I had thought! My lip was very swollen, and so was my nose, as were my eyes, from crying. There was still blood on my face and neck and the girls quickly wet some paper towels and tried to clean me up. They were almost in tears too, when they found out that she had done this to me! I used cool paper towel on my face to try to take out the swelling, but nothing could help this! I had to give the closing prayer during the ceremony looking like this. Oh no!

The girls decided to go with me to the car to get the gowns and stuff out, just in case Mom were still by the car and tried to say anything to me. We lucked out! She was inside already. We got the gowns and stuff out and ran back toward the bathroom but we stopped when Dr. Burgess held his arms out for a big hug. I was embarrassed for him to see me like this, but he was our closest family friend and knew that Mom was a screamer and stuff. He took one look at my face and was shamed for her sake. He told me that he was going to talk to my Dad about this and he told me to call him if anything like this ever happened again. He gave me a big hug before we had to run to get ready for the ceremony to begin. I really needed that hug. I always loved Dr. and Mrs. Burgess because they were always so kind and they always had nice things to say to everyone. Dr. Burgess was very encouraging to me. They felt like a second set of parents to me because I could sit and talk to them like they were. Bud and I went to their house a few times when Mom would loose it and get out of control. Mom would never punish us either. I guess Dr. Burgess would calm her down before she blew up.

Time for the service to begin and we all lined up. I kept my head down and covered my face with my hand, as much as I could, so that no one would see. We had to sit up front on the front two rows in the sanctuary, so that helped a lot. No one could see my face being up there. There was a portion of the ceremony where the students made a presentation to their parents. We had flowers to pin on the fathers and mothers. There was no way that I was going to get up in front of everyone and walk down the aisle and pin a flower on her. No way! When our names were called, Bud got up and grabbed his and my corsage and went back to where she was sitting and, sort of, threw them to her. She was shocked that he had humiliated her like that. Bud had his ways of letting her know how he felt about her without saying a whole lot. She got the point! I was sitting up front but I just had to see what he was doing, so I peeked around and saw everything! I turned back around and laughed silently to myself, but I was screaming like a cheerleader for Bud on the inside. I'm not one to try to set out and hurt anyone's feelings, but she deserved every bit of it this time, and hopefully, she would quit treating us this way if she knew how we felt.

The ceremony was coming to a close and I knew that the time was near for me to show my face for the closing prayer. Thankfully, people close their eyes for prayer, so they would only get a quick glimpse of my face.

Here we go! They're calling for the closing benediction. I stepped up on the platform to the podium, with my head looking downward, and asked everyone to stand for closing prayer. It was obvious that there was something wrong with me without even looking at my face! My lip was so swollen that it made me talk funny. I said a quick prayer and exited quickly to my place. All that was left now, was the march out of the church. This would be easy to hide my face behind the cap with my face downward. Whew! It's over! Oops, I forgot about the standing around and mingling afterwards. I just went to the car and got my things to go to the party, and there she was. She was standing at the car waiting on me to tell me how much Bud had embarrassed her by pitching the flowers at her and as I looked up her, I saw tears in her eyes. I didn't want to make her angry so that she would say that I couldn't go to the party, so I tried to ease her by saying that he just didn't know how to pin them on. I quickly reminded her that we would be back after the party and that I had gotten us a ride home and I ran off before she could say anything further.

This meant that Summer was here again and we would soon be off to Summer Camp again. Bud and I both looked forward to this year and we had even talked Mom and Dad into letting us stay there for two weeks! This year, I would get to ski! I was taking horsemanship and something else too! Bud and I were anxiously waiting for July to arrive so we could go! It proved to be another two best weeks of my life again! There was a sense of peace there at camp. The counselors all seemed to really care about their campers and being good leaders and the instructors were lots of fun, but most fulfilling of all were the campfire worships. I enjoyed singing and all, but there was always lots of fun or funny things that went on at campfire and some deep inspirational stories told. Stories that really made you think about your relationship with God! These were the times that seemed to keep my reigns pulled in to keep me from falling apart at the seams. There were even a few times that I would pull some counselors or teachers aside and ask them to pray for me and I even opened up and told them about the few terrible things that had happened to me thus far and searched them for answers. I always asked them, "Why does God, who is suppose to love me, let these things keep on happening?" They never had THE answer. I had asked many people, during my teenage years, this very same question and they never had THE answer. They would try to tell me that God doesn't like to see anyone have to suffer but we live in a sinful world and therefore suffering takes place, but that answer was not good enough! There had to be a better answer than that! I always looked for someone to give me THE right answer and I'm sure that they just felt that I was searching for pity. Sometimes I was just looking for pity, or love, or attention. I desperately craved approval from any older adult that could tell me that I was OK!

I also desperately craved affection. I was always on the search for a boyfriend. I didn't really care if I ever had female friends, but male friends were very important to me. I hung out with guys much more because I got along better with them. When you hang out with girls, you always seem to be in competition, whether it be for looks, talents, boys, just whatever! That's part of growing up, but it gets stressful. I enjoyed playing with guys and flirting with them and gaining their attention. It was fun! Sometimes, it got me into trouble though. A boy would expect more from me than I was willing to give and I never wanted to lose them because of it, so I would never just come right out and refuse; I would try to put them off for a while or change, the subject.

The attention from a boy drove me to do a very stupid, but fairly normal, teenage stunt. I had met this really cute boy from Camp meeting. He was a doll! I really wanted him to remember me, but how could he, if he lived clear in Oakcliff? His name was Elton. He even had a cool name! There was something about this guy that just made him irresistible. I knew that I would have to keep a little reminder of myself heading in his direction, so I would give him a call occasionally. There was a really big problem with that though. It was long distance! How could I get this phone call to him without being caught! I should have just written him a letter, but my need to hear his voice just one more time was irresistible! I thought that it would be relatively harmless to make a few $.50 calls to him and just have them charged to some other number. It later caught up with me.

I was a very good leader as a teen. I was asked to help out that summer with the Vacation Bible School program that the churches were joining together to do at Burton. I was in charge of the crafts projects for some of the older kids and I really liked taking on those types of responsibilities. Mom was always willing to take me to church and school functions and she was also a dear when I would ask her to give my friends rides. She rarely turned me down when I asked her to pick someone up, especially if it involved church activities.

Even though I have mentioned some very bad traits of hers, it just wouldn't be complete if I didn't mention her good qualities. Mom tried her hardest at doing many things. Any time someone asked for a volunteer for something at church, she would usually be first in line to help out. She was in the choir and took me faithfully every week and even picked up Schantile to go with us. We were always late, but we were always there. She always helped take food when they asked for volunteers and she accepted a position to answer the hotline for the TV show that our church had, but she was always so late that she would only be there for the last few moments. People knew her so well that they just counted on her to be late! She would even take charge of a group of young people for Sabbath afternoon activities by taking us to do Nursing Home ministry or to pass out literature in the neighborhoods. She would then take a lot of the kids home after we finished, if they couldn't get a ride. Melanie, Schantile, Pam and Liz, Deanne and others always liked it that she would take us places. They knew that she had a short fuse, but they didn't know how bad because she was usually pretty nice around them.

She allowed me to start up a girl's singing group called the C.G.A.'s. That stood for Christian Girls in Action! Mom helped us to all have matching dresses to wear by buying lots of coordinating material and she sewed most of them herself because most of the mothers couldn't sew. She was a very talented seamstress. She taught Schantile and me how to sew and we helped her to get the dresses ready. We had two different types of dresses that we wore. The ones that were our least favorites though, were our bee dresses. The material was on clearance at the fabric store and they had three different colors of the bee pattern and we could have our dresses for just a few bucks!$! We decided to go for it but we certainly had to do some talking to the girls to get them to buy our idea. They turned out alright looking, and we did all have matching dresses for only a few dollars, so no one really complained about the bees after all. Mom would play the piano for us at Nursing Homes while we sang to the old folks to brighten up their day. We really liked doing this. We had to practice during the week though, so that we wouldn't sound terrible when we performed. This meant that all the girls would have to come to our house one afternoon each week to prepare and Mom was willing for every one to come over and she would play for us. Mom had to arrange her Piano, Voice and Flute lessons around this group, and she really didn't seem to mind, although she let me know quite often, how much she was doing for me. That seemed to spoil the special feeling of it when she would always remind me of how much she did for me. I always tried to remember to thank her for anything, even if it was to pick up a friend. I forgot occasionally, but I really did appreciate her efforts! I even publicly told our church congregation how much I loved and appreciated all that she did for me and that I knew that she didn't HAVE to do those things. I wanted her to realize that I was very aware that she did FAR more for me than my Mother ever did! Still, there were times that she would either mention her efforts to me again or throw them up in my face about something else. I hated that! It made me feel that I owed her my love. I wanted to show her love and do some nice things for her just because I wanted to, and not because I was always reminded of all that she did!

One afternoon, when the girls were over for practice, Mom needed to get some things done in the kitchen to prepare for dinner and so she asked me to play the piano for the girl's practice until she got finished. She had told us that we had fooled around long enough and that it was time to get busy. She reminded us that she had changed her schedule for us and that we need not waste her time. I wasn't a very good pianist, but I could play out our harmony parts for practice. I started off, playing the soprano notes and the girls still hadn't gotten in the mood to sing. They were still giggling and talking and so I looked at them and whispered, "Come on, let's sing or I'll get yelled at!" They started singing just a little bit more and then something funny happened. Melanie had tripped or stumbled and nearly fell over and so we all started laughing! Mom heard us and she yelled out "Girls!" We turned around to the music again (which was in the opposite direction from the kitchen where she was) and as I started playing the piano again, we were all startled by Mom's bizarre behavior. She had a large butcher knife in her hand and she held it in the air as she came toward us and CHOPPED the knife down on the stack of sheet music that was sitting on the piano, only a foot in front of us!!! The knife blade had come down right in between Melanie and me. We were all white as a sheet and our eyes were about to pop out of our heads as we looked in astonishment! All eyes were staring at the knife! She then demanded that the giggling and fooling around was to stop and that we were to get busy or else they could just all go home! She left and went back to the kitchen and everyone's eyes were still looking as though they had just seen a ghost! One of the girls suddenly remembered that she was supposed to leave early that day, so she called her mom to pick her up. The others were too scared to move, so I started playing the piano again, and they sang, but very quietly.

When we were finished, we all went out front for their mothers to pick them up and Pam and Liz told me that they were NEVER coming back to practice again. They were scared out of their pants! The other girls decided to try to hang in there with me one more time, as long as something like this never happened again. The group wound up breaking up shortly after that because the girls always had some other plans and just couldn't make practice anymore. I wanted to have other plans too, but I lived there!

Those phone calls to Elton, that I had charged to other numbers, finally caught up with me. The phone company traced the pattern of suspicious calls that were all reported to them from various numbers and found that they all went to the same phone number in Oakcilff. They called my house and talked to Mom about the situation and how they had found out that I was the person who was calling this number and charging the calls elsewhere. SHE BLEW UP!!! She called me in from outside and the moment that I stepped into the door I knew that I had been caught for doing something, but she didn't immediately tell me. She grabbed me by my hair, on the crown of my head, and drug me into her bedroom. At this point, I was standing on my feet. She let me go, just long enough to dig the belt out and then the screaming and beating began! BUT, she had grabbed me by my hair again and as she whipped me, she would continue to pull me around the bedroom floor by my hair. I was on the ground now, being drug by my hair because I had fallen after one strike from the belt went across the middle of my back! It took a while for me to figure out why I was being beaten, but I finally was able to comprehend her screaming fury! At this point, I just wanted the beating to stop. My hair was being ripped out with every yank. The raving continued for about 5 minutes. Maybe longer, I would have never known. I knew that I deserved to be punished, but this was closer to torture! When it was finally over, I had been struck on most of my body from my feet to my neck, both sides! I was also trying to get the hair out of my face but it seemed that everything that I was pulling away, was falling out! Oh my gosh, it was!!! Handfuls of it were coming out. My head felt like it was bleeding, it hurt so bad! I ran to my bathroom to look at my wounds. I hated her for this!

I had blown it, but no one deserves this. I deserved to have to pay for the calls, be grounded for a long time, and even spanked, but not terrified to the point that I thought I was going to die! How did they (the phone company) figure this out? They are obviously smarter than I!

I was so embarrassed to return to school. I had NO hair on the crown of my head. The spot was so big that I could not cover it up. It was so sore that I couldn't even try. Monday came, and I had to face everyone. The girls didn't laugh about this, at least. Instead, they tried to help me fix my hair to cover it. It was a source of embarrassment for at least two or three months!!! I learned my lesson the hard way!!! I never made a mistake like that again!

As I said though, Mom wasn't all bad. She still went and picked up my friends to spend the night with me and would take them home and stuff. She would let a whole bunch of them come over at once, if I wasn't in trouble. She even let Schantile and Rhonda come and live at our house for several weeks once when their mother was having a hard time after changing jobs and moving. Their mother often times needed help from others in the church since she was a single mother trying to rear two girls without any help. My mom helped her out often especially if it meant taking care of Rhonda and Schantile. Schantile and I were very close. We were the very best of friends! She always helped me to keep cool about some of the things that I was going through. We knew everything about each other! Every intimate detail was shared about our deepest thoughts. We prayed together every night too, when she was staying with me. We tried to get Rhonda to fit in with us, but her wild streak was even too wild for me!

Mom talked Dad into taking the Pathfinder leader position one year. The church had a difficult time finding leaders that would take on this position because it was quite time-consuming and some people just don't like dealing with teenagers. Pathfinders is a sort of "CO-ED" Christian Boy Scouts and Girl Scouts Organization in the Adventist church throughout the world. I was glad that they were taking the job because this meant that we kids would have more time to be together. Pathfinders had weekly meetings where they had Bible lessons to study and we had to learn different honors. Honors were our patches that we earned to prove that we had sufficiently met all the requirements in a given area, such as knot tying, macramé or camp skills survival. The group also went on a few campouts during the year. We went to Cleburne State Park for our first excursion. It was close to home, but perfect for a short weekend trip. We had lots of fun.

While we were there, I talked Schantile into putting some Hydrogen Peroxide on our hair to lighten it! She was sure that this would make our hair fall out, but I assured her that it was no different than the results you would get by using "Sun-in". That was a well known product that you could just spray on your hair and go out in the sun and the sun would automatically lighten your hair. I told her that the ingredients were similar and were bound to work. She went along with my idea and we drenched our hair in this and sat out in the sun for a few hours. We didn't wash it out until we went home, so it had a long time to work on our hair. By the next day, it was quite obvious that her hair was less resistant to color change than mine because she had a bright, brassy, reddish color now instead of her warm, brown, natural color. My hair lightened some also to a less bright brassy red. Well, I was right! The cheap stuff DID lighten hair! I didn't think about how we would explain the lighter hair to our parents though! We told them that we guessed that we just had sat out in the sun too long. I can't believe they bought it. Schantile, however, wanted to kill me! The next day was picture day at school and she had this new strange color for her school pictures. She only wanted to add a few highlights to her hair, instead, she looked as though she had been to a really cheap hairdresser! She promised me that she would never listen to anymore of my neat ideas!

Mom had tried to find some interesting things to teach us and she decided that we should learn how to bake bread and then we would earn the Baking honor. She bought a bread dough mixer for us and had told us that we would have lots of fun. She invited the girls to spend the night on Saturday night and we would bake bread on Sunday morning. We had lots of fun Saturday night and when Sunday morning came, she woke us up early for breakfast, so we could get it out of the way and begin our bread. This new machine was a manual, hand-cranking type machine, but she told us that it would be a lot of fun. We all looked at each other as if to say that she was an old lady, who got her fun kicks in strange ways! But, we went along with the plan. She got out all the ingredients and taught the girls how to read a recipe and measure properly and clean properly. She didn't miss a step. When we had all the ingredients added, she placed the lid on the pan with the crank, and showed us how to use it. It wasn't real easy to turn after the dough began to form. Each girl would take a turn by turning 20 or 30 rounds and then change off. After the novelty wore off, we were no longer interested in that hard work.

She came up with an idea though that got every single one of us, back into the groove. Now we were even fighting over who would get to turn it next. Her little secret to us was this little chant (as we turned the crank), "We must, we must, we must improve our bust!" All of us were in the "blossoming out" stage and so this sounded great! We all needed a few more inches up there. She told us that this type of exercise was great for increasing our bust line. We all had a great time cranking our bread. When we were finished, we placed the dough in pans and cleaned up while we gave it time to rise. A few hours later, we were all sitting around eating fresh baked, hot bread!

Our next big trip was to Colorado during Spring Break in March. Dad built a special trailer from an old pickup bed and a camper shell, so that we could put all of our gear in it for the trip. Mom had a cabinet maker fill the inside with shelves so that we could make the most from our space. I taped it off and painted it white, with a green strip down it, so that it would match our Ford Econoline window van. Dad had really fixed our van up inside so that we could make the most from it too. He added a bunch of bus seats and he and mom covered them in some new, green vinyl. We could carry about 15 people in there now and it was not a big oversized van. My dad was very clever. It had taken us a long time to get everything prepared for the trip and to get the Pathfinders to get their money ready. As it ended up, Mom and Dad didn't turn any of them down, whether they had money or not. I thought that was very nice of them.

It was time to head out and we left Ft. Worth with 13 Pathfinders, Mom and Dad, and one other Chaperone. Mom and Dad had every stop planned out with an itinerary so full that we barely had time to breathe! We were headed first to the Panhandle to stay at Palo Duro Canyon so that we could see the Outdoor Mountain Theatre Show. It was great! Everything was done on an outdoor stage and the real mountains were the backdrop scenery. The next day we would actually be in Colorado! We had plans to see "Cripple Creek" (an old mining town that was nearly abandoned), "Pikes Peak", "Royal Gorge" and many other sites. There were also some caverns planned on the agenda. They were called "Cave of the Winds". We were even going to climb to the top of "Seven Falls".

We had our little trailer packed full but it was very neat and well organized. Mom was the type of person to draw out organization plans first and then carry the plans with her, like a map. I think that she got a little TOO detailed when she would draw the shapes of everything on the walls so that everyone could know where things belonged. A simple word "CUPS" would have done just fine. Don't get me wrong, I believe in organization fully! (We even had to have our drawers at home organized just like the military! We had to tri-fold our underwear and place them in a neat little row!)

Our nights were very cold up in the high altitude! The guide at "Cave of the Winds" told us girls that we would be warmer sharing the same body heat and therefore the less clothes that we wore inside our bedding, the warmer we would be. We had been so cold the night before that we decided to give this a try tonight. The boys slept in pup tents - two per tent. The girls had one huge tent that easily slept eight people. We all made our sleeping bags into pallets with more sleeping bags for covers and we decided to sleep 3 or 4 girls together. We were toasty warm that night, in spite of the high winds on top of this hill where our camp ground was located. We were really glad that we had met up with that guide who told us about this. Everyone had finally fallen asleep, when we were suddenly awakened by a gust of wind that ripped our tent all the way across the bottom of one side, causing our tent to come down. We were no longer excited about being toasty warm in our beds, because now there were eight girls screaming and running around in bras and panties, trying to find some clothes or sheets to cover up with! The boys thought it was hilarious! We wound up having to sleep, very uncomfortable, in the van that night. Those bus seats were NOT made for sleeping on or under!

The next morning, we had a change in our agenda. Dad had to find a the local yellow pages and find a tent repair shop in the area. We folded up the tent, loaded it in the van and headed into town. Mom was able to make some quick adjustments in our schedule so that we could have something fun to do, while waiting on our tent. We found a little Music Opry Show to watch at Matinee prices. Since there were 16 of us, we had to be very frugal with our money.

The trip had many high points. Mom and Dad had done very well with planning out the activities. The food is another story though. Since we were vegetarians as were several of the other kids, Mom made the menu accordingly. Most of the meals were OK, some were tolerable, but there was one particular meal served, that everyone agreed that they would rather starve than to eat. It was some kind of Chinese Chow Mien. There aren't many kids who like Chow Mien anyway, but when you add diced SOY chicken to it, it makes it even worse! Most of the kids tried to eat it and when they saw an opportunity when Mom wasn't watching, they would go dump it in the trash or over the side of the mountain where she wouldn't find it. If she had found out that they were throwing away food, she would have gone into her spiel about how it is a sin to be wasteful and how she and Dad her had put in their hard earned money so that they could even go on this trip. The guilt trip about how much she was doing again! This made everyone upset when she would start on this. She overheard a few kids grumbling about the food and that started her on her spiel! She started telling everyone how ungrateful they were for what she was doing for them, and that they must be a bunch of spoiled brats, and on, and on, and on! She was really mad now and everyone knew it. Poor little Wes. Wes was a very small boy for his age and the kids always teased him by calling him "Poindexter" because he wore black plastic frame glasses that were always sliding down his tiny nose. He was a small fry deluxe! He had red hair and freckles and that didn't help him out any. He was very smart though and everyone knew it. He was always the MOST obedient of all the kids. That evening, he had really tried to eat the Chinese stuff, but his stomach was really weak, and he couldn't take any more. He knew not to make my Mom mad by saying anything to her, so her went to my dad and said, "Mr. Brandon, do I have to eat any more of this? I feel sick!" My dad felt sorry for him because he didn't really like it either, so he whispered to Wes to go over to the edge and pitch it without Mrs. B. seeing him. Wes looked up at my dad as though he had just saved his life from fire! He wasn't really good at sneaking around, so he looked around to make sure the coast was clear and made a run for the edge of the mountain. If anyone had been watching him and not known what he was about to do, they would have thought that he was about to jump. He meekly walked back toward the camp with his empty plate to throw it in the trash can. He didn't get caught, but when she made a trip to the edge to dump out some old dish water later, she found a slope that had Chinese supper scattered abroad. She was fuming mad!!! Some of the kids tried to explain to her that they really liked it, but had just put too much on their plates and couldn't finish. I guess she half way believed them and that settled her down some. The kids liked being around her when she was calm. They learned to stay clear from her if she was stewing. She was as though a volcano were about to erupt!

The next morning was our morning to pack up and head back home and it was the nightmare of the whole trip. Mom was still a little upset about the previous night's dinner being wasted so she was a little bit snappy. She barked out an order to me to do something and I told her to wait a minute, and I would do it. This set her off to yelling at me and when I turned and asked her to stop yelling at me, she took a swing right for my face! This time, it was an open-handed slap! I am not a slow learner. The last time she did this, I had been slapped so hard that I almost fell off my feet! This time, I made a defensive move to block the blow. I raised my hand and caught her arm right before she hit my face! Boy was she ticked off! Then she looked down at her hand and started yelling that I had just broken her thumb! I didn't break her thumb, I merely blocked and stopped her swing. She ran to my dad telling him how I had broken her thumb. There was only a slight swelling in it, but she assured him that it was broken! She could still move it just fine, but when she showed it to him, she swore that couldn't. I saw her when she was packing up things, using her hand just fine, but when anyone was around, she would pretend that she was incapacitated! She showed it to all my friends, telling them that I had broken her thumb and how rebellious I was. She ran me down from Colorado, all the way to Texas!!! She had just ruined a perfect trip for us all. Everyone was very uncomfortable on the way home, having to listen to her carry on about how ungrateful we all were. There was silence in the van for miles! That made for a very long trip!

Everyone was glad to get home. They all thanked my parents for taking them on the trip, called their parents and left quickly! Even though the trip ended badly, it gave us lots of memories to talk about for a long time. Mom had a nice souvenir to show to everyone at church. Her "broken" thumb. She told everyone she saw about how I was so rebellious that I broke her thumb. She didn't include the part of how she tried to knock the stuffing out of my face!

I was grounded for a month over that incident! I hated being accused and punished for doing something that I didn't do. Dad never said that he believed me or not, but I could tell that he was sick of hearing about her thumb. I tried to explain to him what had really happened and his only response was that I should have never raised my hand to her. I tried to explain over and over that it was self-defense. He stood on his statement.

Since I seemed to get accused of doing things that I didn't do and I would get grounded for this, I started to get an "I don't care" attitude. I started sneaking out of the house at night to see boys all kinds of stuff. I had even started sneaking around smoking cigarettes again. You must understand how stressful it was to try SO hard to make someone love you and trust you and be a hard worker and try to show that you are responsible, and then to be blamed for doing things that you didn't do. This just knocked all my desire to keep trying, in the dirt. Especially, when she criticized me and told everyone in the church what a rebellious and thankless daughter I was. She would then tell them of all the things that she had done for me. I was becoming very bitter towards her. Even though the bitterness was beginning to set in, I would still try to please her at times. It is important for a teen to feel that they are accepted and respected. One way that they can earn freedom and trust is to accomplish a given goal. I needed to feel that my hard work (being good and responsible) was worth it. I didn't want to be showered with gifts, but I needed to feel appreciated. I needed to be PRAISED for anything good. That would give me the desire to do more! I felt that all I ever received was WRATH, and being RUN DOWN, and even HUMILIATED!

Even when I was spending time with my dad, out working on the car or van, she would get jealous and say nasty things to us or give me some kind of work to do for her, to keep us apart. She was very jealous of the time Dad and I spent together. Dad always liked having Bud and me help him work, whether it was on the vehicles, the yard, the house or whatever. Dad even had a plan to teach me how to fix a car for little minor repairs, so that I would never get stranded when I began driving on my own. He taught me how to do a brake job, do a full tune-up, change tires, etc. He even taught me about the full engine and transmission system while he was overhauling the van. I really enjoyed learning about it, but I most enjoyed being with my Dad. It was fun to work with him. I would always laugh at him when he would mash his finger or something like that, cause he always made such a funny face. He would grit his teeth and say some of the funniest things. He RARELY said a curse word, so he would be quite creative and say something strange and we would die laughing. He got mad one time, when he was trying to overhaul the van transmission, because he had worked for hours on this thing and when he put it together, he realized that he had left out a bolt. He turned and kicked it! That is, the transmission. Kicking the transmission didn't help at all, but I sure had to run away and laugh when he started hopping around with his sore toe! I didn't dare laugh where he could see me. He then sat back down and started over again to take the thing apart and figure out his mistake. Mom came out there later on, to see what we were doing and she asked me to come in and help her with dinner. I tried to tell her that I was helping Dad with the van and that I would really like to stay and finish it and then Dad spoke up and told her that he needed me to help hold some things anyway, and that he would like for me to stay. She got so angry that he had gone against her wishes that she started screaming at us how we should be ashamed of our incestuous relationship! This wasn't the first time she had ever said something like that! Dad got really angry at her tacky insults every time we did anything together, and told her that he couldn't believe that she would accuse him of that, just because he needed my help. He then told her that he would have gladly used her help, but that she didn't like getting greasy and working on cars. She continued on in her jealous rage and went back into the house, slamming the door as she went in. Dad just looked at me with his same old puzzled look of disgust and shrugged his shoulders and went on about his work. He told me that he just couldn't understand why she was jealous of his own daughter! She always tried to make our relationship out to be some cheap, dirty, scheming fling. I just wanted her to be proud of me that I was learning about mechanics.

The types of work that she wanted me to do were always cleaning in the house. She always had so much stuff that the house was cluttered. It was clean, but cluttered. The book shelves were so full that you could hardly get a book out and she always like to assign shelf cleaning for me. Or, she would have a big stack of music out on top of the piano, and she would want me to go and file it all away. OH BOY! Just what a girl dreams of!!! More clean-ing!!!

I always had a full load of chores that I did and I knew that if I didn't do them, then no one would get to spend the night with me. I rarely got to spend the night with other girls because she didn't trust me. She didn't think that their parents would keep a close eye on me and then I would be running off with a pack of boys. She always gave me great ideas of bad things to do! There were many times that I put those ideas to use.

I spent the night at Melanie's house one night and when she and her older sister - Tammy, fell asleep, I snuck out to go riding with my boyfriend - Mike. When I tried to sneak back in, I accidentally woke them up! They were startled at first, thinking a stranger was coming in and they almost screamed. Then when they found out that it was me, they were furious! They told me that they would tell their dad on me if I ever did something like that again because they were afraid that they would also get into trouble for my actions. Melanie told me that she was very angry with me for doing something so stupid. I understood her anger and promised her that I would never do that again and begged her to forgive me. Thankfully, she did! I didn't ever want to lose one of my best friends! It took a long time for her to get over it though. I had lost her respect, I knew!

Ninth grade was a better year for me than eighth had been because some of the teasing had stopped. Not all of it though! Not until the big fire!

One afternoon, after Bud and I had walked home from the bus stop, I was upstairs in my room, busy doing something. I knew that Bud was in the playroom (the room next to my bedroom) doing something but I didn't know exactly what and I really didn't care. He had gone back into his bedroom (down at the other end of the upstairs) a few minutes later and he shut his door. I had been talking on the telephone for a few minutes, and when I hung up, I walked out of my room to go downstairs and I saw a stream of black smoke coming from the wall plug in the playroom. It smelled like a real fire too and so I started yelling to get Mom's attention to tell her that the house was on fire. When I got down to the bottom of the stairs, I looked up the ceiling as I heard a strange rumbling noise. I yelled back up the stairs to Bud to get out of the house and I turned and saw Mom coming toward me to see what was going on. For a moment, she thought I was bluffing, but she heard and then smelled it to and ordered me to get out and call the fire department. I yelled back upstairs for Bud and he came out and ran down the stairs. I ran next door and beat on their door to get them to answer so I could use the telephone. It took them too long, so I opened up the front door and yelled at them that I needed the phone because our house was on fire. The lady told me that she would call the fire department for me and to go back and make sure that everyone was out, but she also ordered me to stay out! I went back to see if Mom had come out and I couldn't find her. I could see the blaze on top of the house and I new that it would go quickly since we had wood shingles! I ran in yelling for mom and she was telling me that she had to get the picture albums and she was covering the piano to protect it and she was gathering anything she could get to put on the front lawn to keep safe. The black smoke was now pouring through the downstairs area and I kept crying to her to get out! She ordered me to go out and wave down the fire truck when they came, so that they would know exactly which house it was. How could they miss it with 8 foot blazes coming off the top?!!! I went out and ran down toward the end of the block and they were already coming! They worked fast and furiously and they had to nearly drag Mom out as she was still getting out anything she could grab and she was yelling at them to not get the piano wet! The firemen were having a very difficult time trying to get it under control and she was steadily yelling at them to protect her piano. I was so scared! What would we do now? Dad was gone on the road working, and he knew nothing about it! Several fire trucks responded and they finally got the fire out. By the time we were able to go back and look at the damages, it was almost dark! Her piano had been covered by a tarp and mostly protected. That was her chief concern. I could tell by looking from the back yard, that there wasn't anything left of my bedroom. Bud's room was mostly gone, but furniture was spared. There was a lot a damage from the water, more so than the fire, and even more damage from the smoke!

Chapter 6: Wild Child!

Time came, and Mom and Dad drove us down to the Valley. It seemed like the drive would never be over. It took 12 long hours. But when the moment came for us to send them back home, it seemed all worthwhile! We arrived on the same day as the Seniors graduation night. This meant that there were still lots of students there and that there was no room to unpack our things until the following day. They had to have us camp out in the little Chapel. Schantile, Melanie and I stuck close together. Schantile's oldest sister, Cynthia, was there and was graduating that night, so we went to say hello to her find out her plans for the evening. She was going out for the night with her boyfriend. "Going out!", I said. "I want to go too!" Cynthia told me that I wasn't old enough to go where they were going and to keep quiet about their plans.

Her boyfriend's friend was looking for a date to go out with them that night and he asked Cynthia to ask me if I wanted to go with him? Wow! He was asking ME out? He was 20 years old! How cool! A 20 year old asking out a 15 year old. This was great. Cynthia told me that I couldn't breathe a word of this to anyone, so I kept absolutely quiet and was at our meeting place 10 minutes early to be picked up. When I saw my date, that I hadn't met until this point, except from a 50 yard distant glance, I realized that he might have a difficult time getting a girl. He wasn't drop-dead ugly, but he wasn't a looker either! It didn't matter to me though, because I was out for fun and excitement. Just imagine! My second night there, and I'm already out on a date with a 20 year old and we're off to Reynosa, Mexico (a little border town, just across the Mexican Border)!

As we got out of the truck, the guys warned us to stay right with them, because we could easily get into serious trouble in this town. They weren't talking about the Policia either! We went to a bar and the guys ordered drinks. The asked me what I wanted, but I wasn't really sure, since I had only tasted a beer before when Mother took me with her to bars in Temple. I asked Cynthia what she was having and so I just ordered the same. It was some type of Rum and Coke mixture like they had been drinking on the way down there. This bar was a dive. It wasn't the type of place that I had dreamed of going to for a date, let me tell you! They kept announcing in Spanish about a Senora that would be out in a few moments and the guys told us that this meant they were going to have some lady dancers. Well, was I ever shocked!!! The ladies, (if that's what you'd call them) came out topless! They were fat and ugly too! The guys with us watched for only a few minutes and they agreed that they were even too ugly for them. We left and went and walked around for a while, looking for another place, but believe it or not, that was their top-notch, hot spot! We decided to leave and I had no idea where we were going now. After two of those drinks, I didn't much care either. When we got back into the truck, my date asked me if I wanted another drink. When I told him that I really didn't, they started to make fun of me and I quickly changed my mind and took the bottle and drank a big drink! Straight Rum! I took another just to look like I wasn't a baby. We had to drive for a whole hour back to Weslaco, but I was totally passed out after 30 minutes. This date kept trying to kiss me, but I wasn't really wanting to kiss him since I didn't know him and when I passed out, he just kept right on. I didn't wake up until we had arrived at Weslaco and Cynthia shook me. She said that she needed to tell her Dad good-bye before he left, and since I was drunk, I couldn't go along. Her boyfriend suggested that they drop us (me and my date) off at the city park to wait for us. The way that I felt, that sounded great to me! I could lie there and sleep just as well. The date told me that it was after park hours and that we had to hide or we would get caught by police, so we had to hide behind the bushes. While we were hiding, he actually tried to undress me! I was fully awake now and I told him that I would scream if he persisted, but he insisted that I had wanted this all along! What? I never asked for this! I was struggling with him when some headlights appeared. They were the police! I looked at this guy sternly and told him that I would scream rape, if he dared to touch me again. Since the police were just on the other side of the bushes from us, he agreed to my demand. I was hoping that they would stay for a while, but they left. This idiot tried to start kissing me again, and I managed to get up and start walking away, when Cynthia and her boyfriend returned. What a wonderful sight! They drove me back to the campus and Cynthia walked me up to the door, just 20 steps from where I had to lie down. It was 2:15am, when I walked in and Schantile was waiting for me. I stumbled in and she nearly died when she smelled me. I was reeking of cigarette smoke and Rum. I lay down and told her where we had gone and was giggling for a few minutes. She kept shushing me to keep me from waking up the others. Suddenly, I felt sick! "Schantile!" "Help me!" I begged! "I'm going to be sick." She was yelling at me in a whisper, "Not in here, this is the Chapel!" She got up and dragged me to the bathroom, where I threw my guts up! Boy did I feel better. She was so mad at me! She told me that she wasn't going to be my friend down there if that's what I went there to do. She didn't want to have any part with me drinking and smoking. I told her that I was very sorry and that I really wished that I hadn't gone with them and told her how that guy nearly raped me. She told me that she would forgive me as long as I promised, on the Bible, to never do that again. I promised!

The next morning came way too soon. Schantile woke me and told me to get to the restroom quickly and brush my teeth again because I smelled like a brewery and she didn't want anyone to find out what I had done! Neither did I, so I quickly ran down to tidy up. Schantile went with me and when I looked in the mirror, I was in horror! Oh my gosh! Look at my neck! It was covered in hickeys!!! I never even knew that this had happened! I remembered him trying to kiss me a few times while I was passed out in the truck, but I thought that I had pushed him away mostly. Schantile looked at me with a very disappointing look. I felt so embarrassed even for her to see this. What was I going to do now??? I couldn't possibly be seen with these things on me, but there were so many, that I didn't know where to begin. Make-up!!! I got my make-up and began applying a very thick coat. All of my attempts to cover didn't do very much to covering. I had some zinc-oxide with me and so I tried putting that on and then some more make-up on top of that. That was little better, but you could still see them. They were red, and purple and covered my entire neck. I looked like I had been mauled!! Schantile offered for me to wear her brown blouse that had a matching scarf to tie around my neck and maybe that would hide them. I couldn't thank her enough!! I tried it on, and tied the scarf on and it looked much better, I had to be very careful not to move my neck much, because the scarf had to be fully extended to cover the majority of the area. It still didn't cover it all, but at least it wasn't blaring obvious anymore. Only a really tall turtleneck would have covered a little better, but then I would have looked like and idiot in 100 degree weather, wearing a turtleneck!

We had already missed breakfast, which I wasn't crying about since my stomach was churning, and so we decided to go walk around and see what was going on. There were very few people here now. They left right after graduation or early that morning. It was scarce! We found a few kids hanging out in the gym so we sat in there for a while. Everyone kept staring at us! I was so worried that someone would see my neck, so I didn't go up and talk to anyone like I normally would. Wow! It's lunch time and we were starved now. We went in and found a light lunch that was very tasty. We learned that the cook's name was Mr. Dickerson. He was a very good cook! We later learned that his cinnamon rolls were the most sought after in the whole

Adventist Conference! There wasn't anything that I had ever eaten that even came close!!

After lunch, we went back into the gym. We had to wait a day or two to get our work duty assignments. Schantile wanted to work at the Nursing Home. Yuck! I couldn't take the Nursing Home smell for that long. I enjoyed singing and visiting there but not for a job. We looked at the positions that were open on the list that was posted and I quickly found the job that I wanted! Lifeguard! I had earned my Senior Lifeguard at the YMCA the summer before and now I could earn money to use it. I checked out the swimming pool and found that it had been drained. I later found that they had made a few repairs and had intended upon opening it later that week. I was going to have to do another job also, to make sure that I got in enough hours to cover my school bill. The pool hours were from 3:00pm - 10:00pm so I had a lot of time to work another job or even two. I saw a part time Office position open and that was another area that I was really interested in, but it was only for 4 hours a day. So I decided that I could also handle some dormitory cleaning in the mornings from 7:00am - 10:00am. I could run straight from the dorm to the Office to work from 10:00am - 2:00pm.

I had my plans all mapped out. I was called in to see the Summer Dean. I asked Schantile if she had been called in too, but she hadn't. I wondered if this was normal.

She introduced herself to me as Margo and told me that she had just arrived too and was the Summer Dean. She started looking at my neck and I looked down in shame and was trying to hide it. I certainly didn't want her to know about this, it wouldn't make for a good start there. I didn't want her to think that I was a bad girl. She asked me in a very kind tone, what had happened to my neck. I respectfully told her that I didn't really want to talk about it. She asked me where I had been the night before, and now I thought that someone had told her. I asked her who had been talking to her and she told me that no one had, but she was a little bit concerned about me. She had such a tender voice. She told me that I could talk to her about anything I ever needed, and that she was there to help if I ever needed it. She asked me one more time about my neck and for some reason, I felt as though I could open up and tell her. She was so very understanding! She didn't put me down or scorn me or anything like that. She just gave me a big hug and told me how sorry she was that I had made a few bad choices, but that she wasn't going to tell about it this time, BUT, she made me promise her that I would never get into that type of situation again and that I would really try to be good for her so that I wouldn't make her look bad. Wow! She was so cool that I didn't want to ever do anything to hurt her. It seemed like a great summer was in store.

I wound up getting all of the jobs that I had applied for and it would seem that this would be enough work to keep anyone out of trouble! 16 hours a day! But, I got off at 10:00pm and I was ready to play. I started sneaking off campus with some new friends after I had been there a few weeks. Bud did too! We often ran into each other out in the town at some hang out. I found a new boyfriend almost immediately. His name was Joey. He was 16 years old. He lived in town and drove a pickup. The only time that we could really spend together was on Sabbath afternoons and this was never enough. He would come by and visit me at the pool and that was when we began making plans to meet after 10:00pm. The girl's dorm was locked by 10:30pm. The Girl's Dean kept a pretty close watch from 9:00pm-10:30pm to make sure that no boys came in to spend the night with a girl. The Boy's Dean would do the same. 11:00pm was bed check time. Everyone had to be in his own room by this time, unless previous arrangements were made. The Dean checked with a small flashlight to see that everyone was in bed. I always made it back in, just in time.

Joey had been invited to a big party and he wanted me to go with him. It was a late night party and he knew that I had to be in at 10:30, so we made plans for me to sneak out that night. I had heard that other girls had done it before, and it shouldn't be that difficult. I had done it a few times back home and had only been caught once. (That was when we lived in that rent house and when I didn't shut the front door all the way, trying to keep Mom from hearing, the wind blew it opened.) The plans were to stuff the bed to look as though I were in it asleep so that we could leave at 10:30 instead of 11:15. He would meet me out back with his truck parked nearby and then he would bring me back later. I had made sure that a window, on the back side of the dorm, was left unlocked so that I could get back in.

It worked! We were off for the party! We had a great time and he brought me back at 2:00am. Joey went up to the window with me to help me open it and take off the screen and replace it. We were very quiet! Just like professionals! We slipped off the screen, opened the window, he kissed me good-bye and helped me in. When we were pulling the window back down, a little flash light came on right beside me!!! "Who's there!!!" I whispered. "It's just me," Margo answered in a whisper. It felt as though all my blood had just rushed out of my feet! She then thanked me for showing her how it's done and how good we were at it. She opened the window and told me to call Joey back. She told me that we were both to meet with her and the boys dean out on the front porch in two minutes. We attempted to get a story together during our dreaded walk to the meeting.

Dale (the Boy's Dean) was out front waiting with her and they both sat down and calmly asked us to be seated. There was no use in trying to lie to them. We just both looked at them and surrendered, "We're caught!" I spoke up and told Margo that I was very sorry that I had broken her trust and I knew that I deserved a really big punishment. I just asked her to tell me what it was and to get it over with.

They were really surprised by our admission of guilt and thanked us for the truth. They made a deal with us! Only because we were truthful! Margo gave me some in-house punishment and that meant that I had no privileges for two weeks and that if I kept my word, then they would not tell Mr. Kruger. Mr. Kruger was the school Principal. If Mr. Kruger knew about this, I would have been expelled, they informed me.

We felt very fortunate for their merciful kindness to us and I never snuck out again. I did everything I could to show Margo that I appreciated her lenience. The only bad thing I ever did past that was to sneak off campus during the day for 30 minutes or an hour. I would go shopping or riding around with another guy that lived in the village. (The students that lived in the area were called Village kids.) Joey and I had already broken up just a few weeks after we had snuck off. I wouldn't have sex with him anymore. I let him talk me into it one time, even though I didn't really want to, but was too scared that he would break up with me if I didn't. I was trying to be good, but this was not something that he was interested in, so he didn't have anything to do with me after that. Terry was from the village and he was so much fun. He had a little VW bug and he taught me how to drive it. I already knew a little bit about driving a stick shift, but I wasn't very good at it. He was patient with me and would keep letting me drive around a little while in the village. He started liking Rhonda and I thought that was great! We all hung out together during my time off.

I really enjoyed working at the pool, although a few weeks after I had begun the job, I had my nose broken while horsing around in the pool. I was dunking a girl, but when she went under the water, her knee came up and hit me right in the nose. They had to take me to hospital and the following morning a doctor operated on my nose. Schantile went with me to the hospital to keep me company and to help me out. I had never had any type of surgery before and I was really scared. Schantile was right there! She stayed there the entire time. I couldn't have ever asked for a better friend. She told me that they were going to pick up a new student at the airport just before they picked me up. I didn't know anything about this new student and was a little embarrassed to meet anyone looking like I did. I had tape on my face and bloody bandages. They came in and removed the bandages and packing and I was only going to leave with a little splint. I was bruised though and Schantile was scared to clean the old dried blood off my face because she was afraid to hurt me.

When Margo and Dale came to pick me up, they brought the new student with them. It was a guy! I wanted to crawl under the sheets. I couldn't believe that I had to meet a guy the way I looked. Oh well! He was really nice about it. His name was Lindy. He later became one of my very best friends. He had asked me to go steady with him, but we tried that for a while and I just didn't feel right about it. I asked him if we could go back to being friends. He had been so nice to me and even agreed to stay friends. This was very unusual because most people say they'll be friends and then turn around and never speak to you again.

I accidentally hurt him just weeks before school started. The girls and guys would always play pranks on each other from one dorm to the other. This one night, the girls decided to go turn off the lights to the boys dorm. It was so funny! I was elected to do the dirty job. I loved it! I had to sneak over to their electrical box, which was located in an adjacent building that was still under construction, and I pulled the lever, cutting off their power. I ran back as fast as I could so that I wouldn't get caught before the girl's door got locked! We were all watching from the windows as the guys started hollering out their windows about getting even with us. We saw Lindy come out of the dorm and walk over toward the building where the box was to turn the electricity back on. We overheard a yell and saw a spark, but didn't think that there was any problem. The next thing we knew, the boy's dean was running over to the building along with several guys and we heard sirens within moments! Word got to our dean, that Lindy had been electrocuted! He was knocked out from the jolt and had been thrown across the room. I couldn't understand how this could have happened. It was perfectly safe to simply lift the lever. It was harmless! How did he get electrocuted? We found out that he didn't know anything about electricity and he opened up the box to feel around for a switch and that is why he had been shocked! There was a foot of water on the concrete slab floor, from an earlier rain storm and when he opened the box, he touched bare wires!!!

I wanted to go see him!!! I was screaming and crying! I felt so responsible! If I just hadn't gone and turned off the electricity, then none of this would have happened. Margo wouldn't let me out of the dorm because the ambulance people didn't need me in the way. I asked her to see if he was going to be alright and so she told me that she would check as long as I stayed inside. She found that he was conscious and able to talk, but unable to move his right arm and leg. They rushed him to the Emergency Room.

I had a difficult time falling asleep that night for fear that I had severely injured anyone, much less, one of my best friends.

The next day, around noon, he came walking up to me, with his arm in a sling. I jumped up to give him a hug and told him over and over and over, how sorry I was. He said that he didn't blame me, but felt stupid himself for not knowing what he was doing. I asked him what was wrong with him arm and he told me that it was paralyzed. "PARALYZED!", I screamed! He told me that the doctor said that it might be temporary, but he wasn't sure. He seemed so calm! I vowed to him to do anything to take care of him and to do his homework and anything else he needed.

I began praying and praying that God would heal his arm and within a week, he had almost full use of his arm again. What a relief!! I thanked God many times and even told Lindy that I knew that God had healed him.

I couldn't believe that he remained my friend through all of this.

Summer was closing and the school was getting ready for another school year. Registrations were coming in to the office and schedules being made. Since I was there during the summer, I had first pick at several things.

The night before the "Howdy Night" (the Saturday night get-acquainted party before classes were to begin), a village guy that I had met just a few days before, came up and asked me if I had anyone to go with. I told him that I didn't know anything about it and certainly hadn't been asked by anyone, so he asked me if I would like to go with him? I couldn't believe my ears!!! This guy, Kurt, was one of the finest guys in the whole school and a Senior too! I had been informed by some other girls who were "in the know" about the guys there that he was a Doctor's son and that there were several girls that liked him. I immediately told him that I would be honored to go with him and I asked him what all "Howdy Night" was about (so I would know what to expect). I COULDN'T BELIEVE IT!!! I WAS GOING TO ATTEND THE PARTY WITH THE HOTTEST GUY IN SCHOOL!!!) I thought that he was really cute! He looked like a surfer-type guy. He had shoulder length blonde hair and a dark tan. He wasn't big and muscular, but cute and sexy! He drove a sporty little car too!

We attended the party together and he asked me to step outside with him to cool off for a minute. The gym was a little bit warm in the hot summer. He held my hand and began walking around the side of the building. He stopped and looked into my eyes for a moment and then, he kissed me! His glasses got in the way and so he took them off, and kissed me again! Wow! Could he kiss or what? I had never felt like this before in my whole life. I had been kissed many times before, but this was something like you only dream of. I felt like a Princess being kissed by a handsome Prince. He then asked me if I would go steady with him? I was now totally overwhelmed!!! I thought that I needed to pinch myself to make sure that this was real. With a very surprised and stunned look and voice, I stupidly asked him, "Are you sure that you want to go with me?" He said that he wouldn't have asked if he didn't mean it and so I quickly accepted. I kissed him this time and then he spoke up and said that we had better get back inside before they came looking for us. I floated all the way back. We were holding hands when we entered the building and I was as proud of myself as I could be. I was actually going steady with the finest guy in school. I couldn't wait to tell Schantile. I told her that this guy was really special and that I was going to do everything right with him. She warned me that I needed to be careful, but congratulated me too! I quickly got back to his side!

The evening ended way too quickly! I didn't want the clock to ever strike 11:00 to end the party, but it did. I had to tear myself from him after he kissed me good-bye. This was the best evening of my life! I could hardly go to sleep for talking about my new boyfriend. Schantile and the girls were tired of hearing about it and told me to go to sleep. I lay in my bed, still in disbelief. Nothing this good had ever happened to me before. I felt like I was in love with a Charming Prince, but everything seemed too good to be true! I didn't feel good enough to go with such an awesome guy. I wondered what he saw in me to ask me to go with him? I was no beauty and certainly didn't measure up to him. I had this question running through my mind all night as I finally fell asleep.

The next morning, I had to go ask Schantile if it was true, that I was going with Kurt? I wanted to make sure that it wasn't a dream. This was Sunday. I didn't know if he would be around that day or not. I got my dorm cleaning done and went to work at the pool at noon.

I only hoped that he would appear some time that day to see me, but there had been no plans made. My day seemed so much brighter as I sat on my perch (the lifeguard chair) and recounted the events of the night before.

Around 5:00pm, I caught a glimpse of Kurt's car. He came to visit me for just a little while before he had to be home. He assured me that he would see me the next day at school. I knew that we wouldn't see each other too much though, because he was a Senior and I was a Junior. He told me that he was going to try to get a campus job the next day and then he could see me a little more often. He knew that they were still hiring some guys for construction on the unfinished building that was going to be an auditorium and used for Chorale.

The next day was our first official day of classes. I was forced to make one major change to my schedule of classes. I had signed up to take Chemistry, but when the teacher began talking about how this class was based on Algebra, I realized that I wouldn't survive. I had only barely passed Algebra at Burton because I never understood Mr. Newton's explanations. I asked him many questions, but he seemed to talk in circles, leaving me even more confused than before I had asked! Had Dante, Melanie, Debra and Larry not helped me, I would have never even passed. I had no clue what we were doing! There was no way I could pass Chemistry if you needed Algebra as a basis. The teacher gave us an opportunity to ask if we had any questions after his brief overview of his Chemistry Class. I raised my hand and asked,

"How long do we have to sit in a class before we drop it and choose something else to take?" He pointed the way to the door and said that I was welcome to leave right then! I decided that I should go right then and get a schedule change.

I enjoyed my other classes. I was even taking shorthand because I thought that I might later become a secretary. It was hard, but fun.

Terry (the guy with the VW) and Kurt were really good friends, so Kurt and I always hung out with Rhonda and Terry. Kurt was a good student in school like I was, but Rhonda and Terry both had some lazy attitudes about school. Rhonda had always had a bad attitude about school but Terry was actually smart. He was just in a mood and tired of school for a while.

One day only about 6 weeks after school had begun, Rhonda and Terry had gotten into trouble about walking around campus holding hands and Kurt and I had already gotten that lecture just a few days prior to that. We were told that we were spending too much time together. I couldn't believe that they would tell us something like that as long as we weren't getting into trouble. At least none that they were aware of. I'm not saying that we were sneaking out at night, but we did leave campus often during the day, to hang out. They didn't even know about that though, because we had never been caught! All four of us sat down at one of the picnic tables out on the lawn and began talking. We were saying how we were sick of being hassled by everyone and how nice it would be to be on our own. Terry seemed to have the right answer. He said that we should just all leave. We could go away and make it on our own. We talked about where we would like to go if we ever did run away and we started talking more seriously. We talked about how we would make money and live and that we would have to get married. Talk turned into real plans. We all decided right then, that the next day, we would leave and run off to Las Vegas, where we could get married, and then find us a job in California maybe. We could make this work. Kurt had a good car, and had $780.00 in his bank account and this would be enough to finance our endeavors, until we were able to get a job. I told them that we could stop off in Abilene where my Mother lived and spend the night there the first night. We could just tell her that we were on a "Fall Break" and she would never know the difference. I knew she wouldn't call Mom and Dad and tell them. We had our plans all mapped out and we were going to leave the next morning right before the first class.

I really had to sneak around to pack my stuff without my room mate knowing what I was doing. I was clever though and she never had a clue. When she left out the next morning, I only had to pack the remainder of my things and I was ready to go by 8:00am. I went to eat breakfast and to find Rhonda to make sure that she was ready. I couldn't find her, so I ate quickly and went back to her room to look for her. I found her alright, but she was NOT ready to go. She hadn't packed a thing! I quickly started rounding up her things and then she told me that she wasn't going. "NOT GOING!", I said! "What do you mean?" She told me that she was going to chicken out but that she didn't know how to tell Terry. I begged her to go but she was sure. I was hoping that this wouldn't change everyone else's mind. We gathered at our appointed meeting spot, and I had to drag Rhonda there so she could tell Terry face to face. He was very disappointed, but still wanted to go. We all agreed that we still wanted to go, so I ran to my room and then put my suitcases in the car and asked Kurt if I could run to tell Schantile good-bye. I ran and got her from class and told her about our plans, gave her a hug and told her good-bye. She could only say that she hoped we knew what we were doing and we said good-bye. I swore that I would write to her real soon!

I ran and jumped into the car and we were off. No one had a clue! Kurt said that we had to make a stop in San Benito first to go by his bank and withdrew his savings. We were really scared that they might get suspicious and call the police since we were emptying his account. We thought that $780 was a lot of money to them, but we were just overly paranoid! We had no idea if the school realized that we had gone yet, so we didn't waste any time getting out of there.

We drove straight to Abilene. We got there around 6:00pm and told Mother and her new husband, Harvey, that we were on Fall Break for a week. They believed us, just like I told them they would. We told them that we were going to Colorado on a ski trip with several other classmates that would be meeting us there and we would have to leave early in the morning.

She fixed us a little breakfast and we wasted no time in leaving. We drove to Albuquerque. We decided to drive around the neighborhoods and see if maybe we would rather live there. We could still drive to Las Vegas in a few days and get married if we could just find a job and an apartment. We stopped by the Apartment Locators office and found out that housing costs were extremely high in this town. We quickly changed our minds about this place and headed on to Vegas.

We drove for several more hours. I fell asleep during this long boring drive and Kurt woke me up as we arrived at Hoover Dam. He wanted to stop and get out and look at this site since we were passing by. We got out and he told me why Hoover Dam was significant and it was kind of chilly in the night air, so we were only there a few minutes. After getting through the canyon area, I could the Vegas horizon. We had made it! We were actually there!

The drive in to town was breathtaking. The place was so lit up that it seemed like daytime. We decided to stop at a motel that looked like one we could afford and Kurt told us to stay in the car while he went in to pay. He thought that they would be less suspicious that way. Terry had been talking about "Wanted Posters" and stuff as we entered town and how he was worried that his dad already had private eyes looking for us. Since we were runaways, we had to be very careful. Terry was 18 years old, Kurt was 17 and I was only 15, but I had a fake ID card that showed that I was 18! Kurt went in to check the room prices and Terry and I waited outside by the car in the parking lot. We had been there for about 10 minutes and a car pulled up beside us. Two men got out and approached us showing us a badge and asked us for our ID's. They asked us how old we were and what we were doing and we told them that we were 18 and just visiting. We told them that our friend was inside getting us a room. Kurt came out while they were looking at our ID's and then they asked him for his. He showed it to them and they told us that since Kurt was only 17, he would have to stay inside. We were informed of the curfew law and it was long past. All minors had to be off the streets by midnight! They handed us our ID's back and left. We all nearly fainted from shock AND disbelief that they believed us and didn't arrest us. We were so glad that they had not checked us out. We took all of our stuff up to the room and as soon as we got in, Terry told us that he wanted to go walk around and check things out. We reminded him to be careful and he told us that he would be back in an hour or so.

We had a chance to laugh at how I was allowed to go out on the streets but Kurt couldn't since he was only 17! That fake ID sure came in handy! We were tired from the trip and fell asleep within a few minutes.

We woke up at about 8:00am the next morning when we saw the rays of sun coming in through the curtain. I looked over at Terry's bed and saw that it was still made up. I sat up quickly and told Kurt that something happened to Terry. Then, we saw a little piece of paper on his pillow. He had left a note stating:

"I guess that you realize by now that I split. I got worried about my dad looking for me and decided to fly home. Sorry Kurt, but I had to borrow $350 to pay for the plane ticket home. I promise that I won't tell anyone where you are and Good Luck!"

Kurt jumped up quickly and found his wallet and c ounted the money. It had already taken about $150 for food, gas and one night's stay in this room and there was only nearly $300 left! Kurt was SO mad! "How could he do this to us?" he yelled! "Now how are we going to make it on this small amount?" We looked at each other knowing that we were in big trouble! He suggested that we go to breakfast and ask around about jobs. We knew that we would have to get jobs immediately in order to keep from running out of money before we would get our first paychecks. I told him that I could do waitress work and we could get tips to help us out. That sounded pretty good to him.

We found an inexpensive place to eat nearby and we ordered something light and sat and talked. We had a hard time eating with the worries we had on our minds. Kurt started telling me that he knew that Terry wouldn't keep quiet about where we were and he felt that the cops would know where we were before the day was over. He said that we didn't have enough money to go somewhere else to live because it would take more gas. Kurt sat quiet for a few moments and then looked up at me and said, "Maybe we should go back." He then told me that he didn't want to feel like a criminal on the run and even said that if we called them first, then maybe we wouldn't get into so much trouble. I thought for a minute as we held each other's hand. I didn't want to have to run scared either and I didn't want to live out of a car, SO, it seemed like his idea was the only solution! He felt that it would be best to call his parents first. We told them that we had a change of plans and that we were heading home, but only if they agreed not to call my parents until AFTER we got there. They agreed to our request and so we went back to the room, packed up, and headed home. We had a very long drive ahead of us.

It wasn't nearly so much fun driving back, in fact, it was quite stressful. I knew that I was going to be dead after this stunt! I could only wonder what

they would do to me. I knew that I deseverved the worst. I was just hoping that somehow, I wouldn't be separated from Kurt! We really loved each other. We talked all the way home about how we wouldn't let this keep us from getting married later on. We were definitely getting married, some day!

When we arrived at Kurt's house, his parents came out and gave him a hug and said that they were very happy that he had decided to come home. They didn't have very much to say to me and I could only guess the horrible things that they were thinking. I'm sure that they felt that it was my fault that their son had done something like this and that I must be a little tramp! Soon as we went inside, they told us that they had kept their bargain about calling my parents, but that they had notified the school so that they wouldn't have the police still searching. They told us that they were calling the school to come and pick me up.

The Principal and his wife came to get me and they told me that they had already made arrangements for me to have a flight home. They had just called my parents and told them a few minutes before they left to get me, and they were taking me straight to the airport. Wow! I hadn't even had time to return to school. I asked them what was going to happen to me and they told me that they would call later, with their decision. They had to meet with other faculty from the school before they made their decision. I talked to them on the way to the airport and told them that I was very sorry for disappointing them and that we had learned a big lesson. I told them that if they would even consider giving me another chance, I would never disappoint them again! They listened and said that they would relay my message to the other faculty.

I got on the plane and felt sick. How could I face my parents! What would they do and what would they think of me now? The plane ride home was very short. I never wanted it to land. I just couldn't face them. I knew there would be no hug for me when I got off the plane.

I walked down the ramp to the entrance of the airport and met my Dad before I got out of the ramp. He took me by the arm and told me that he hoped that I no ideas about running from him because if I did, I would regret it. I assured him that I wasn't going to run. He then said the worst thing that I could have ever heard! He told me that he was ashamed of me and regretted the day that he ever adopted me. He looked broken and crushed. I told him that I was so sorry that I hurt him, and he said that he didn't believe me. He even said that he didn't know what to do with me and he even called me a tramp. I just cried. He then asked me if I had slept with Kurt. I tried to tell him that we only shared a bed together but we didn't have sex. He told me that he didn't believe me. I felt very uncomfortable with these questions, but I knew that I deserved it. When we got home, he told me to go straight to my room and that I had better not try to sneak off or even pick up the phone and I assured him that nothing would happen.

I took a few minutes to write them a letter of apology to let them know that I knew that I had made a really poor choice, but that now I had learned my lesson and I was ready to do what was right. I had even assured them that I would make it up to them and make them proud of me from then on. I then hoped that it would ease their pain.

The school notified us, a few days later, that I was to be suspended for two weeks and that I would be allowed to return after Christmas Break as long as I agreed to be on permanent social bounds from Kurt. Dad told me their decision but he also said that he wasn't sure if he was going to let me go back. After three weeks, Dad sat down with me and told me that he would give me another chance if I would agree to their terms about being social bound from Kurt. He told me that he never wanted me to speak to him again! I agreed to anything, just as long as I could go back. I was just sure that they would change their minds after a little while, if we were good!

When I returned, the first thing I did was call Kurt at home. They didn't say that we couldn't talk on the telephone. He told me that he loved me and how much he had missed me, but he also said that he didn't ever want anyone to see us together because he didn't want to be kicked out during his Senior year.

We tried really hard to be very discrete! We wrote lots of letters and talked on the phone mostly. We knew that the school faculty knew that we were still engaged. When the Valentine Banquet came up, we decided to go together, but we would sit across from each other, which still violated our 20 foot boundary. We felt that we had done really well for the past 6 weeks and surely they wouldn't bother us for sitting across the table from each other. Well, no one separated us. Maybe they never noticed.

We loosened up about being so discrete when we saw each other hoping that they had just forgotten about everything.

Well, about two weeks later, I was called into the Principal's Office. I was not forewarned about what this would be about, but all of a sudden, I had a sick feeling. My worst nightmare had come true. I was being expelled. I asked why, and I was informed that they were told that I had been smoking Marijuana in the girl's restroom by the classrooms. I hadn't though !!! I insistently refuted their accusations!!! I told them that I had NOT been smoking anything in the bathrooms, but the more I talked, the less convinced they were. I couldn't believe this. I was being accused of doing something that I hadn't even done. Now, it's not as though I had never smoked any since I had been there, but the very few times that I did, I didn't do very much. I didn't even like the stuff and certainly wouldn't risk getting kicked out of school over it. I was innocent and I told them that I was really upset that they believed this lie. They told me that they were also not happy about my social bound restrictions. They told me that I hadn't followed them as they had told me to. I told them that I had really tried, but I knew that I was guilty of that. But I didn't feel like they should kick me out. I had done better since I had come back, and I didn't smoke any marijuana in any restroom. They had already made up their minds before I went in. I told them that I wanted to call my mother in Abilene because I just couldn't possibly go back home to Mom and Dad with something like this. There was no way that they would believe that I was innocent if the school didn't.

I called Mother and luckily, she was home. I asked her if I could come and live with her since I was getting kicked out of school. She said that she would be down there the next day to pick me up, so I packed up to leave. I didn't really want to live there, but I didn't want to live with Mom and Dad after being accused of smoking marijuana. There was no way that they would believe me. I had done too much to spoil my reputation and this would just bury me.

Mother and her husband - Harvey, picked me up the following day and we drove to Abilene. I cried all the way there because I was so upset about leaving Kurt. We vowed to stay faithful to each other and he promised to come and see me soon. Mother believed me when I told her that somebody had to have lied about me just to get me into trouble. She seemed very different than when I lived with her last.

We arrived at Abilene and Mother took me, the next day to check into school. Here we go again. Another new school. I knew absolutely no one except Bud. Bud had just moved there the month previously because he didn't like the Valley school anymore. I think that he had also gotten into trouble and he didn't want to be around Bee anymore either. So this was different! Mother was very lenient now. She didn't care if we smoked, drank or anything, just as long as we went to school. So, I took up smoking full time. I was already a part time smoker from being around Kurt and Terry, but now I could smoke without hiding. I smoked a pack a day.

The very first week that I was there, I was invited to a party. I was really glad to be asked, so that I could meet some friends. Mother didn't mind at all. She just asked that I be home by 12:00 midnight. Some friend from school came by and picked me up and there were several others in the car too. We drove out to the county for a Bon-fire! It sounded like it would be a lot of fun and there were supposed to be a lot of people there. Not long after I got there, I was shown where the keg was and I poured myself a very small drink. I didn't like the taste of beer at all and there was nothing else there. We were out in the country, with no houses around for miles. I was trying to mingle and some guys walked up and asked me if I wanted to smoke some weed? Weed is just another word for Marijuana. I tried to politely decline their offer, by telling them that I had done that stuff a million times and had never gotten high from it, so I didn't want anymore. They had a great come-back line, "Oh! You must have never tried this, cause this stuff is the real thing. It will waste you!" Well, I thought that it wouldn't hurt to take a few puffs just to be polite like I had always done before. I didn't want to get high, I just wanted to meet new friends. They told me to come to their car with them and they would fire it up. The car was full of people, but I was the only girl. Oh great! I was hoping that I wasn't in for something else. I tried to sit by the door, but I got pushed to the middle. These guys had a thing called a "Water Bong" to smoke this stuff. I had seen people use one before, and had taken one puff before, but I didn't want to stick around this time. I started to get out by telling them that I could barely breathe from all the smoke, but they handed me this pipe and told me to take a hit. I tried to just take a little puff (or hit as it's commonly called) but they were able to tell that I didn't get any, so they told me to try again. Well, after a long inhalation, I got choked from the overwhelming amount of smoke that I got. I started coughing and they told me to take another one before I left. Well, if taking just one more would get them to let me out, then I was all for that. I took one more hit and thanked them for it (just to be polite) and walked away. I had only taken about 10 steps and was trying to talk to the girl that gave me a ride, so that I could find out what time we were leaving, but suddenly, I felt impaired. I couldn't hold myself up. I couldn't even talk! I was so unsteady that I nearly fell into the bon-fire just trying to sit down. I literally could not move or even think! I felt like a ZOMBIE! (At least that was how I always thought a Zombie had been described!) I was not able to function! I sat in front of the fire for the remainder of the party and some friends had to load me into the car to take me home. I kept hearing everyone saying that I was really messed up! I just wanted the feeling to go away. I didn't like not being in control. As they began to drive me home, I became slightly more oriented. I was even able to partially tell them how to get to my house when we were a few blocks away. Some guy helped me to the door, but didn't want to be seen so he quickly ran back to the car. I was so scared to walk in. I didn't know who would be awake. I was home on time though! I was even 10 minutes early! I walked in and everyone was up watching TV. Oh great! I made it to the nearest chair and just sat down and stared at the TV, hoping no one would ask me how the party went. Well, Mother just had to ask and I looked at her and laughed and told her that it was fine. She could tell by my eyes that I had been into something, but she just thought I had been drinking. She asked me how many drinks I had and I told her, "Just Two!" She and Harvey died laughing and so did Bud! I told them that I wasn't really counting, but that I didn't feel too hot and would just like to go to bed. They said good night and I was gone.

Oh was I ever glad to lie down. That was so scary! I had no idea what they had given to me, but I certainly learned to be more careful who I partied with. You see, that is not the kind of party I really wanted to go to, but that was all that was offered, so I went. I always seemed to land in a pile of trouble!

I had to get up and go to school the next day, but made it OK. I was just a little slow.

The next week, I began applying for jobs. I got one at Long John Silver's and was supposed to start the next week. I got my uniform and everything. Before I started the job, a few bad things started happening at home. Mother and Harvey were getting into drunken brawls and Bud and I were having to deal with them at nights. Harvey was telling Bud and I that he knew "JO-JO". He told Bud that JO-JO lived at the cemetery and even made Bud go talk to him one night. Bud told me that he thought that Harvey was a crazy man and to be really careful around him. I think Bud was right. He did several weird things around the house like howl a few times and stuff. But, when he hit Mother one night, I got angry and called the Police! The police came and told them that they couldn't do anything about it because it was a civil problem and I was furious. I couldn't believe that they couldn't make him leave for the night. The police left without doing anything except advising them to stay away from each other for the night. Harvey went back to bed and fell asleep. Bud and I had not gotten much sleep that night before school the next day. I couldn't believe that I was back in this mess again. I didn't know which was worse: some of mom's beatings and accusations or being a baby sitter for two drunks! I decided that neither was. I had only worked a day, when I decided to call a friend from Ft. Worth that had some really nice parents. Her name was Karen and her parents already knew about how life was at my house with Mom. They had always told me that I could come and stay with them anytime. When I called them, they told me that if I could get a ride to Ft. Worth, they would let me stay with them. The next day, I packed my stuff and called my adult cousin, Sheila, to ask her to give me a ride to the bus station. I told her that I just couldn't handle their drinking anymore and I needed to leave. She was also aware of the situation at home with Mom and so she told me that she understood the situation that I was in and that she would give me a ride, as long and Mother didn't know.

She dropped me off and I thanked her for the ride and rode a lonely bus ride to Ft. Worth. I wondered if things would be better for me at Karen's house. I just hoped that her parents would really keep me around like they had said. They picked me up from the bus station in downtown Ft. Worth and took me home with them. I told them about all my experiences since they had last seen me to get them all caught up. It was Friday evening and they told me that they were going to church the next morning, but that they would understand if I didn't want to go with them since Mom and Dad also attended there. I stayed behind and just wished that I could have gone with them to visit my old friends.

That night their doorbell rang, and to my surprise, my parents were standing there. Her mom came in and told me that she didn't know how they had found out but that she wasn't going to lie for me. Oh no! Now what! I walked out and asked them if I could live there with Karen's family but my Dad told me that I was either going to live with him or my mother. He added that if I was going to live with him, then I was going to follow their rules.

OK! We'll try again!

The next day, my dad sat down with me and asked me what my intentions were. He wanted me to get my education and so did I. He knew that I had problems living in the same house with Mom so he made a suggestion. He asked me if I wanted to try out Jefferson Academy? That was clear out in East Texas! Well, it sounded better than living with Mom, so I agreed. Dad checked into sending me there and took me out there just a few days later. Another new school. Dad warned me as he left that this was my last chance and that I had better make it work.

It lasted a whole month! When I got there, I found my very best male friend sitting on the steps at the cafeteria. LINDY! WOW, I couldn't believe it! We talked for ever and caught up the latest news. His arm was fine now and he still loved me. I told him once again that I could never be his girl friend. I told him that going steady with him would be like dating my brother. It just wasn't right. Besides, I was still engaged to Kurt! I told him that Kurt had bought me an engagement watch (which is an Adventist tradition for engaged couples) on Valentine's Day and gave it to me at the banquet before I got kicked out.

The end of school was nearing and a very important event was approaching. That was, the College days for all the high school student seniors to attend at SAC (Southwestern Adventist College) in Keene. That was so close to Ft. Worth. I called Kurt to make sure that he was going to be there and he told me that he was. I told him that somehow, I would manage to be there.

I told Lindy that I was going to hitch hike there and back that weekend. I knew that there would not be many faculty left there and if no one missed me for the week end, I would never get caught. After all, there were going to be several students gone that weekend. They would just think that I had gone home.

Lindy told me that there was no way, he was going to let me hitch hike to Keene alone. I told him that I just couldn't miss out on the opportunity to see Kurt one more time and that he would be so close!!! Lindy decided that if I was going to go, then he was going with me to make sure that I would be alright. He had family that lived in Keene that we could stay with, so I agreed to take him along. I was actually really glad, because I was scared to hitch hike alone. I had heard some gruesome stories about girls that hitch hiked and were found dead. But surely that would never happen to me!

We made it! We wound up walking for a long ways to the highway and nearly got caught by the most gullible faculty member that saw us on the freeway, but he believed us when we told him that we had missed our bus in Jefferson and had to catch it in Marshall. He dropped us off in Marshall without a single question, and we found someone at the bus station with a CB radio to connect us with a west-bound trucker. We were very lucky to find a trucker who was going straight to Brandom Kitchen in Keene, Tx. We only had to walk two blocks from there to be at Lindy's relative's house.I found Kurt the next day at the college, but my parents also found me there, later that evening. UH OH! This was the end of the line for me!

Chapter 7: Decisions, Decisions

I had to face a few hard facts by now, since Jefferson Academy immediately withdrew me from their enrollment.

Fact #1: It was apparent that I would now be living at home.

Fact #2: It was apparent that I could not practice self control on my own. I was literally destroying myself with every decision I made. The desire to feel loved overpowered my desire to meet parental approval.

Fact #3: I was still in love with Kurt and was scared of the thought of losing him, which was almost certain to happen with a 500 mile distance between us.

Fact #4: Changes had to be made! I could not continue down this path any longer.

Dad went to Jefferson to pick up the rest of my belongings and told me he needed to seek help in having me placed into a reform school. Mom had been threatening this idea ever since we moved in with her and had a few disagreements. But! When Dad said this, I was scared. He asked me what my intentions were for my life. I was really honest with him and told him that I wanted to finish high school and then go to college and that some day I hoped to marry Kurt. He didn't ever want to hear his name again, but I was honest with him and told him that I loved him. He told me that there was to be no communication with him, at least for now. He felt that he was a bad influence on me. He asked me to straighten up and he even told me that if I would finish high school, he would help me get a car and get into college. He was trying to get me to look at reality and have something to work towards. I asked him if he still loved me, and he told me honestly that I was making it very difficult for him to love me, but that he still did. He also told me that he had come to the end of his rope and didn't know what else to do with me.

He then asked me if I could stay out of trouble long enough to finish high school there at the public school - Southwest High? He told me that I was definitely not going to any more boarding academies. The cost was too high for me to keep getting kicked out all the time. He told me that he understood that it was hard to live there with Mom and that was why he had agreed to let us go to the Valley, but that now it was just going to have to work out and that he expected me to get along with her regardless!

The straight talk helped. It helped, for the most part, just hearing him say that he KNEW that Mom was hard to live with. He said that things were better between them while we were down there, because we got on her nerves and she would fly off the handle when we don't do everything just the way she liked.

I told him that I would never let him down again, and that I would work very hard to graduate with good grades. I was then enrolled at Southwest, with only two months and one week remaining in the year. I had the counselor look over my transcript and tell me what I had to have to graduate. My schedule was set. Another new school!

The only 2 people that I knew in the whole school was a girl from down the street - Laurie, and Mike. He was my former boyfriend for about three years. We went steady, off and on, (mostly off) during those years because I would never give him what he wanted. He finally broke my will. He told me that we were going to marry some day, anyway, and that if I didn't trust him enough, then our plans to marry would be off! I certainly didn't want him to break up with me again, so I yielded, in return for his love. At the age of 15 1/2. It had been just months before I had left for the Valley and I had been crushed when he broke up with me only weeks later because I turned him down again. He had taken my entire future, in a matter of a few minutes, and acted as though I was just lucky to be his girlfriend. I'm sure that he had never given me another thought after he broke up with me. That was one of the reasons that I was so glad to leave for the Valley, so that I wouldn't have to think about him all the time.

I knew that we would eventually run into each other. I had asked around about him and wanted to know if he was still seeing the girl that he dumped me for. Naturally, he wasn't. He was well known by most of the girls in the school. I didn't really care about him now anyway, I was in love with Kurt and we were getting married.

I couldn't focus on him now. I just had to keep my mind on one thing, finishing high school. I found some information about taking home study courses from this little job that I had. I worked for a company who sent out the home study packets. I started making plans with my counselor at high school, to take two home study courses in the summer, and a full load for one trimester during my Senior year, and I would be finished! The only thing that would be left for me to do would be to walk down the aisle at the graduation ceremony in June 1978! The counselor told me that, as long as I had all of my credits on my transcript, I would be able to attend the Junior College and start my college education early. That sounded terrific! I now had something to work toward and I would feel really good about myself if I were in college before the rest of my classmates.

I received a devastating letter about a month after starting at Southwest. When I saw the name on the envelope, I just started crying. For the past three nights, I had dreamed that Kurt was breaking up with me. Every morning when I woke up, remembering the dream and having tears in my eyes, I would just tell myself that it was only a dream. I feared that this letter was the reality and as I read it, I learned that I was right. He told me that he just couldn't keep up our relationship without ever seeing me. The hundreds of miles between us had done it. Physical separation really does cause emotional separation. I cried for a week. I knew that if he could just hang in there until September, that then we could begin seeing each other again if he went to college in Keene. He had plans to attend. I wrote him with that suggestion, but his reply was to wait and see once he got here. I later found out that another girl was interested in him and began flirting with him while I was away. The only hope that I had was to wait for September!

I stayed out of trouble for several months. Five months later, when I was almost finished with my high school classes, I did something else wrong. It wasn't as bad as my other stupid stunts, but still wrong. Mom and Dad had to meet and approve of any boy that I wanted to date before I could go out with him. Dad had three basic rules: No long hair (which was in style at the time), no smoking, and no drinking. He told me that if they did any of those things, then I shouldn't even waste my time because the answer would be "NO!" The smoking and drinking rule seemed reasonable, but it was difficult to find a guy that didn't smoke. The hair rule was where we didn't see eye to eye. My hair was only touching my shoulders, and Dad told me that he never wanted to get confused. He just thought that long hair looked trashy on a guy. So I rarely found anyone who pleased me and would also please my Dad. I didn't want to put any guy through meeting Mom either. The fifth degree questioner!

A friend of mine, Mary, invited me to spend the night with her one week end because her boyfriend had a friend that wanted to go out with me. I asked her if he knew me, but she said that she had told him about me already and that he wanted to go out. Well this seemed pretty safe, so I asked if I could spend the night. I hadn't spent the night with anyone since I had been home. Mom said that I could but that she would call and check up on me and that I had better be there. "OK!", I told her.

I thought that we could time it, just right, that Mom wouldn't know we were even gone. Mary thought that her Mother would cover for us anyway, so we called them and made plans. I talked to him on the telephone earlier that day and he sounded pretty quiet. I asked Mary if she had ever met him before and she told me that she had. I wanted a description! What did he look like, etc.? She stumbled somewhat and told me that it had been a while and she didn't really remember. That's great! Sound's like a cover-up for an ugly mug! She assured me that he wasn't a dog or anything, she just couldn't really describe him. I agreed to the blind date and so did he. I had never had a blind date before and this was really scary!

I spent two whole hours getting ready; my hair, my makeup (that I was never allowed to wear at home), and I borrowed one of Mary's dresses AND my ears. Yes they were clean, but Mom had made me quit wearing my pierced earrings and so the holes had closed. Well, I just had to wear a pair of ear rings on a date, so that meant that I would have to make new holes! I got Mary's largest sewing needle that she had in the house and a piece of ice and went to work. Slowly I pricked and pricked and then stopped and applied ice for a while, then went back with the needle. This went on for an hour before I had them both finished. I had almost given up on this, but it was just too important. By now, I had learned the old saying, "No pain - No gain!" Was this ever true! The pain, that is! Mary had a beautiful dress that she loaned me. It was black and sleeveless and had a long apron scarf hem (which meant that it looked like several "V" shapes hanging down). It was very elegant. She loaned me the perfect high heeled shoes AND the perfect ear rings. She helped me with my make-up and hair. I felt like a princess in her beautiful clothes. Mom would never let me own anything like this!

The guys were right on time. The doorbell rang and in walked one that I got a glimpse of through the crack in the kitchen door. I asked her if he was my date and she peeked around the corner to see and quickly turned back to say,

"NO! HE'S MINE!" I heard them talking but couldn't see the other guy. Her date's name was Eddy. I walked out to meet my date. "Eddy was very cute", I thought, "but not very well dressed for a date", and I couldn't see my date anywhere. Mary spoke up and said, "Ray, Meet Cathy!" Then, a shorter guy stepped from behind Eddy and stepped forward to shake my hand. I was so embarrassed! I thought that I was taller than he was with my high heels on, but when we stood on level ground later, we saw that we were equal. He was only 5'9". I was 5'61/2" and with 2 1/2" heels, we were even. I looked him over quickly. He was obviously a Cowboy, judging by at his strange western pants and solid rust colored western snap shirt. He was also wearing old cowboy boots. His hair was below his collar, but not too long. He wasn't ugly, but I had reservations about him. He wasn't dressed as nicely as I would have preferred, but then, we didn't discuss this prior to our date. I was definitely overdressed, but Mary was too, so I felt better. We told her Mother good-bye and that we would be in by midnight. Mary promised me that she had talked to her mother about my mom and that she would cover for me if Mom called while we were gone.

We were only going out to eat and to see a movie. About 5 minutes after we had left, Ray and Eddy lit up a joint! (That is also known as a Marijuana cigarette.) I wasn't very happy to see this, but I kept quiet. Mary even smoked a little, but I passed. Then Ray told Eddy to pull over on the side of the road! I was wondering what was going on when finally Ray told Eddy that he had to go by the side of the road. Well, that's not how a country boy puts it, but you understand his urgency! I thought that he was really rude, but when he got back into the truck, he apologized for not being able to wait any longer. He was too embarrassed to ask to go at Mary's house. I accepted his explanation and decided not to hold it against him.

We ate at a seafood restaurant on Old HWY 80 called "The Wharf" and the food was great! "This was a very nice place for a date", I thought to myself, but I was wondering if he had helped in the planning. He gave me a nice compliment as we were waiting for our table about how nice I looked. That was really sweet. We were so nervous while we were there. We were both really trying to watch our table manners and etiquette. We quickly learned that we both smoked cigarettes and that helped us to find something in common. I hadn't smoked much since I had left Mother's, so I was real cautious about smoking too heavily. I didn't want to choke and I really didn't want to smell like an ashtray!

We left the restaurant in time to get to the movie that was about a 25 minute drive away. The movie starred Henry Winkler. He played a mental patient and the movie was a love story. I really enjoyed it. That is, what Ray would let me see of it. He kept on kissing me. Probably 20 times during the movie. I was flattered that he liked me, but he was going overboard. When we left there, we had to drive straight back to Mary's house so that we wouldn't get into trouble. We were 15 minutes late, but Mary explained to her Mom and we didn't get into trouble.

When Mary and I lay down in bed that night, we talked for an hour. I didn't know why, but there was something about this guy that I liked. I couldn't go to sleep that night for about 2 hours because I couldn't get him off my mind. I wondered if he really liked me or if he just always kissed girls like that on a first date.

That morning, after we woke up, Mary called Eddy to see if Ray had said anything about me. Eddy said that Ray had told him that he really liked me a lot and wanted to call me if I wanted him to. I gave Mary permission to give him my phone number. I still couldn't figure out why I couldn't get him off my mind!

Mom and Dad picked me up later that morning to go with them to church. I was hoping that she wouldn't notice that my ear lobes were still a bit red.

Ray called me that evening and I asked him if he would like to come over. He told me that he could come over for a few minutes and so he did. I warned him that he couldn't smell like smoke when he got there and he told me that he wouldn't.

I told Mom and Dad that I had met him over at Mary's house when they stopped by for a few minutes to visit Mary. Dad said that he wouldn't mind meeting him as long as he met the 3 rules. (No long hair, Smoking and Drinking)

He was very polite when he came over and we just sat and talked for a little while. He didn't stay for too long because we were running out of things to say. He told me that he would call me in the next day or so. He called me every night the first week. He didn't say a whole lot when he called, but at least I wasn't chasing him. By Thursday night, he was already asking me to go steady with him. I thought that it was too soon, but I didn't want to hurt his feelings and say "No" so I told him that I would give him an answer the next day. I didn't want to tell him that I was already going steady with a guy named Doug and I certainly didn't want my parents to know that Doug and I were going steady. My dad hated him! Doug was about 23 years old and had long hair and had a terrible reputation for being into drinking and drugs and lots of trouble. My mom had known him for years because he and Stan hung out together. I called Doug the next day and broke up with him so that I could accept Ray's proposal. I knew that Doug and I didn't have a good future together anyway. He wouldn't stop smoking Marijuana for anybody! We never went out on any dates anyway. We just saw each other occasionally if I were visiting his house on Sabbath afternoons. Friday night, Ray asked if he could come to see me. I told him that I would go steady with him. He was happy, but I wasn't sure if I was doing the right thing. I didn't like going with someone, but I didn't want to hurt their feelings. I didn't think that he would call me again if I had asked him to wait a few weeks and then ask me again.

Oh well! It's done now. Mom and Dad let me go out with him as long as I was back home on time. I met his parents and brothers and sister that next night, and I could tell that they weren't real thrilled with me either. His step-mother seemed "chilly" but his Dad was warm and kind. His Dad was a new Believer! He told me all about his strange conversion experience and how he was a drinking fighter and dope smoker before the Lord changed him. I really liked listening to him talk about God. I was hearing about God in a very different light. I was use to hearing about a God that had a bunch of rules and that you must live up to them or be damned! His Dad, was telling me about a God that would seek someone out and deliver them from their past and make a new person out of them, thus taking the work out it. He explained to me that I didn't have to work to change myself, but that the Holy Spirit would do that for me if that was really what I wanted.

I had enjoyed the evening so much that I couldn't wait to go back and talk to his dad some more. His step-mother, told me that she believed in God and went to church too, but she seemed very "course" for a Christian woman. She was still smoking Marijuana and cursing and I just didn't see the "light" in her, that I saw in his Dad. The words that he spoke drew me and I wanted to listen and learn more. I quickly found that they were of a very different religion and that our church was totally against a "Spirit-Filled" "Tongue-

126

talking" church doctrine. I had heard some Adventist talk about this as being from the "Devil". When Ray's dad asked me what church I went to and I told him that I was an Adventist, he was very polite to not say anything bad about it.

I finished high school in the first half of November and Dad helped me to get a car. He had bought Stan a 67 Mustang, Fastback when he graduated a few years earlier and Stan wrecked it in just a few weeks. Dad swore, after that, that he would never buy anyone else a car. We would have to pay for our own so that we would appreciate it. He was willing to help though. Dad found another 67 Mustang rear end (not a fastback style though) and told me that if I would help him put the two together, that I could have a nice car for only $500.00 and a paint job. When all the pieces were put together, it was three colors; red, green and primer gray spots everywhere. I had it painted a beautiful light blue color with a sparkle to it. I was so proud of it. Dad taught me how to drive it out by Granbury Lake. He didn't want me to be in any traffic since I had to learn how to drive a stick shift. He was so patient to sit through the many times that I killed it before I could actually make it go. I learned very fast though. It only took that one day, and I was ready.

Since I was finished with high school, I had some new freedoms. I already had a job at the Sizzler Steak House for about a week before I got the car because I needed a pay check to get the car painted and to put some money down on my insurance. As long as I let them know my work schedule, I could stay out till 11:00 pm during the week and I had to be in by midnight on weekends unless there was a very special event, for which I needed to get permission first. This was great!

It worked out well for the first week, but Mom started sniffing me down every night when I would come in and accuse me of smoking. I had really been trying to never smoke anymore and rarely did, and when she would accuse me anyway, I would get very angry and hostile. I told her that I may as well start smoking if she was going to accuse me of doing it anyway. She never believed anything I ever said.

Ray and I dated for 6 months and had only broken up once during that time, for just a few days. His dad was pretty helpful to get us back together after he had heard what had caused the break-up. Ray had gotten angry with me, when I got drunk at his birthday party, that was at his house. His parents were gone for the weekend and had given him permission to have the party since he was turning 18. He was nice to ask Bud to come with me and I was later, glad that he had, because Bud had to drive me home. I had never intended to get drunk, but Ray had decided to give me the cold shoulder that night and so I got angry and started drinking a little bit of everything there. I was definitely not cut out to drink because I got drunk very easily and then got sick. Ray had been drinking alot AND smoking pot, so he was messed up too. I had embarrassed him when he found out that I was throwing up and couldn't walk and I thought that he was going to kill me! I stumbled into his bedroom, where he was talking with some guys and told him that I was tired of sitting on my own, without him, and he threw me on his bed, pinned me down, doubled up his fist and reared back to punch me, when his friend Lee stopped him and pulled him off of me. He told me that I was an embarrassment to him and he wanted me out of there. Bud overheard the problem and loaded me into my car and drove me home.

I had bought my own telephone line for my room, and was buying some of my own clothes and was feeling very independent now. January came and I had started college so I was rarely even home. I tried to stay away the entire time so that I wouldn't have to go through the 50 million questions.

Dad's approval of Ray ended in February after he stood me up for our usual Friday night date. I had been sitting in my bedroom waiting for his call. It was already past 7:00 pm and he had usually called me by now. I sat patiently in my room, all dressed up, with hot rollers in my hair, just waiting for him to say that he was on his way and I could finish my hair. I got a call at 7:40 pm but it wasn't from him. An Arlington police officer asked me if I knew someone called Ray. Oh My Gosh!!! What happened. The police officer tried to calm me quickly because he had only had a flat tire and was broken down on the side of the road without a jack. He asked me if I could meet him with a jack. I told him that I would be right there and he told me where he was. I wondered what he was doing near Arlington. That wasn't on the way to my house.

When I found him on the side of the road, I wondered whose car he was driving. When I asked him, he told me that he had a bought a new (used) car and I was mad at him for not telling me about it. He told me that he was on his way to see his cousin, Rick in Arlington, and that they were going to go out. WHAT??? "Why didn't you call me and tell me about this sooner?", I asked. Continuing on, I told him that he was very inconsiderate for leaving me sitting by the telephone knowing that we always went out on Friday night. He told me that his cousin had called and invited him to go out and that he had just forgotten to call.

He fixed his tire and asked me if I wanted a ride in his new car. I thought that maybe he was going to include me in his plans for the evening now, but I was in for another surprise. He took me for a two mile drive and dropped me back at my car and told me good-bye. I was fuming!!! How dare he! To call me to have me drive 20 miles just so that he could borrow my jack!! When I got home, my dad asked me what happened? When I told him, he was furious too. He told me that I was justified in feeling used and feeling that he was inconsiderate. He told me that he hoped that I was finished with him. Dad took the time to sit down with me and talk to me about not letting any boy run over me and treat me rudely. He assured me that I could do better than that and deserved to have someone who would respect me. He told me that if a boy would do something like while we were dating, then he would do worse than this if we were married. I really appreciated Dad talking with me and listened to his advice carefully. The next morning, I got a phone call from Ray. He told me that he had wrecked his car that night on the icy roads and that it was totaled. Inside I was laughing and thinking that he deserved it for not treating me nicely or taking my advice about the ice warning. I asked him if he had been high or drinking and he got angry that I even asked, but I knew that this was the reason that he went to his cousin's. His cousin was well known for all the drugs he used. I told him that I didn't like being stood up and he apologized, and he said that he understood that he hadn't taken me into consideration when he made his plans. He told me that he would call me next time, if he planned on going elsewhere on our date night. I forgave him. Dad was listening to me while I was talking with Ray on the phone. When I hung up, he told me that I was crazy. He told me that he no longer had any respect for Ray since he had treated his daughter like that. It felt very nice to hear my dad say that. I felt that he was feeling proud of me again and wanted the best for me.

Ray and I continued dating after that, but this was only the beginning of some of our disagreements. I was trying to get him to settle down more (actually, I wanted him to quit smoking pot). We also had a few other disagreements about him being inconsiderate to me about other things, as well. But, even though we had disagreements, we stayed together.

That next weekend, I asked Dad if I could go to Keene to go to church. I told him that I wanted to visit there a few times and that maybe I would meet someone better for me. I knew that I told Ray that everything was OK, but it really wasn't. I knew that Dad was right and thought that I shouldn't be too exclusive anymore. After all, we weren't engaged. While I was visiting at Keene, I ran into Kurt. Our eyes caught each others and when I saw his smile, I ran into his arms. My head was spinning with all kinds of thoughts. I was cautious though, because I didn't know if he had any commitments to someone else. We spent the entire day together. I felt like a princess again. Being with him always made me feel so special. He seemed different to-wards me now though. I just thought that the time apart had caused this and that maybe it would get better. I asked him if we could go out together that night to go dancing. I told him that Mom and Dad didn't check on me very much now, as long as I was in on time. Kurt agreed to go out and we went to a place called the "Daily Double". It was a little Disco Night Club. Disco music was THE music of that era. The hottest movie out, a few months prior, was "Saturday Night Fever." While we there, just sitting and listening to music together, my favorite song came on. It was the love song from that movie. John Travolta fell in love with his dance partner and they danced to a very romantic song. Kurt asked me to dance. (Just what I was waiting for.) When we got out to the dance floor, it was empty. The lights were low and the sparkle ball was turning and as we began dancing, it started feeling as though we had taken the place of the John Travolta and his leading lady. We were the only ones on the floor and Kurt's eyes kept looking at me just like he used to, when we were in love. Wow! What a dance. For a few moments, I felt like the star of the movie AND the star of his heart again.

We didn't get to stay there for long, because I had to make sure that I was home on time. When we parted, I asked him when we could see each other again, and he told me that he didn't really know. He told me that he wasn't ready to jump back into a commitment yet and I knew that this night didn't mean the same for him as it had for me. When I drove home, I could only hope that I would know soon, if he ever intended to see me again someday, because I was now feeling a bit guilty for going out with him since I was still going out with Ray.

Kurt and I only saw each other two times after that night. Once, just a few weeks later and another time, right before he left college for summer break. It just wasn't meant to be.

I kept seeing Ray and visiting with his family. I had talked with his dad on many occasions since we had met and during our conversations we spoke about my home life. In fact, he got to know more about Mom first hand because she called over there a few times to check up on me, but would eventually tell Ray's dad all about her problems and how she and Dad had a lousy sex life and all sorts of things. Ray's dad could tell that she was strange. He felt sorry for me having to live with her. He knew that I loved my Dad dearly, but that Dad was gone during the week and it was always during the week that she would get obnoxious!

One evening, I had come in and was on time, and she started accusing me of smoking and drinking and all kinds of things. I had just been at Ray's with his family eating dinner and playing cards with them. I had done nothing wrong, but she was going off the deep end with sniffing me down and swearing that I had been smoking. I told her that his parents smoked and that was why I smelled like it, but she would not believe me. I got upset with her and told her that I was going to spend the night at Ray's house and I would be home the next morning to explain this to Dad. Ray's dad and Ray's Stepmom had already told me that I could spend the night there anytime and they would just let me sleep on the couch, so I felt that this would be a good idea for the night. After all, I was in college, working and staying out of trouble and I still couldn't make her happy! I felt like giving up!

I was home very early the next morning and when Dad came in, I made sure that I explained the situation first. He understood how she could be, but he told me that he didn't want me staying at Ray's house. He felt that I should work it out with Mom and stay at home. Mom began giving her side of the story to Dad and told him that I was screaming at her and she totally blew everything out of proportion and told him that she just wouldn't put up with me being able to leave for the night if we had a disagreement.

I could never talk sensibly to her. I felt that she should start treating me like an adult since I was in college now, but she still wanted to check up on every move I made.

This happened two more times and Dad finally told me that I was to never spend the night at his parent's home again. I was to just learn to deal with Mom and that was that.

I had talked to his parents a few other times about the situations at home and they told me that if I wanted to, I could come and live with them. They understood that she was a wild woman and that I was living in an impossible situation.

By April, I had been through enough. I couldn't take it anymore. I was trying harder and harder and she was nagging more and more.

I decided to leave home. I first talked with his parents to make sure that I could live there and they told me that they would like for me to wait until after the weekend, if possible, because they were going to be out of town. I thanked them for their offer and told them that I was going to move in. Ray and I had talked about moving out on our own and getting an apartment together, but I told him that I didn't want to live with him unless we were married. I didn't want our relationship to be cheap. He told me that he wasn't ready to do that and so I understood that it just wasn't time yet. I felt that we would get married some day soon though.

I decided to talk to Dad about moving in with Ray's family and I told them that they had offered. Dad was angry with me for asking and told me that I was just going to have to learn to get along with her and that was his final decision. He told me that if I ever did move out, then he would NEVER let me move back in, that I would have burned my bridge behind me. He told me that he understood that we had a hard time together, but I was just going to have to learn how to live with her and to do what she wanted me to do. He also explained to me that he didn't want to leave her to help out Bud and me, because we would be gone soon and then he would be lonely. He told me that they get along fairly well when we aren't there and he had something to look forward to, MAYBE! I understood Dad's request and decision and knew that I would have to accept it or move out forever.

I wasn't sure exactly when I was going to move in, but one Thursday night, Mom had embarrassed me again, so I left home and stayed at his parents house again. I knew that Dad was going to be angry, but I also felt that he would understand my side of the story about this situation. The next morning, I tried to talk to Dad about what had occurred but he didn't get home before I had to leave for work. When I finally got to talk to him, it was late that evening. Mom had already told her side of the story and he impatiently listened to my excuse but told me that it wasn't good enough this time. He told me that I was to never stay over there again and since I had done it anyway, then he was going to take my keys and my telephone away.

Well, I didn't think that this was fair at all since I was paying for them. This meant that I was going to have to move out now. I couldn't go back to being grounded from my car and all, so when I went to work, I called Ray and asked him to get me later that night. I knew that mom would be busy with company from church that night and that she would never miss me!

I grabbed only a nightgown, tooth brush and tooth paste, and I was gone! This was Sunday night and we hoped that his parents wouldn't get angry that I had been there while they were gone. They were supposed to return that next afternoon.

The next morning, Ray had to go to work. He worked for his Grandfather and Uncle at their tire shop. He left for work and I stayed at his house. I was in the house near a window and I saw my Dad drive up. OH NO!!! I didn't want him to find me there alone. He would kill me. He obviously knew that I had left home because he looked really angry! He went up to the front door and was beating on the door really loudly and looking into the windows to see if anyone was inside and I could hear him yelling, "Cathy, I know you're in there, now come out here or I'm coming in!" I ran into the bathroom and when I heard him come in the front door, I jumped out of the bathroom window and ran down the street to Eddy's house and stayed with his sisters, Betty and JoAnn. I was petrified! I only hoped that Dad hadn't seen me run away. About a half hour later, the girls walked up there to see if my dad had left and they came back to report that he was gone. I called Ray at work and told him what had happened and he just asked me to stay with Betty and Jo Ann until he or his parents came home.

When his parents returned, we explained to them what had happened and shortly after they arrived, my dad called. He asked to speak to me. I didn't want to talk to him because I was scared. But I had to, because I was going to have to tell him that I was never coming back home. I took the phone and said, "Hello Dad." He told me that I was never to call him Dad again. He told me that he had now disowned me and that I should come and get my stuff off the front porch, because he would have a "Goodwill" truck come by and get it if I didn't. He told me that he hoped that I had made a decision that I could live with because I had now burned the bridges. I hung up crying. I never wanted to hurt my Dad. I only wanted to get away from Mom. I wasn't even in love with Ray, but I needed to get away from Mom and his parents had offered a solution that I thought I could live with. When I hung up, my Dad's words raced through my mind over and over again, "I disown you and never call me Dad again!" HAD I MADE THE RIGHT DECISION?

Chapter 8: Freedom at last!?!

I didn't want to think about it any longer. I just wanted to get busy and get on with my new life. I had still been working at Sizzler Steak House and I was still in college at TCJC. The college was only two miles from Ray's house so I asked Ray's step mom if she would agree to take me to my classes. I had called in sick that Monday, when I had left home. My boss was not happy that I called in sick at the last minute but I had not thought about this new problem. I didn't have a ride to work, therefore, calling in sick seemed to be the only solution. The next morning, I was supposed to be at work at 11:00 am. I didn't want to put his parents out by asking them for a ride everywhere, so I called in again and tried to explain my situation to them. The boss got on the telephone and told me that if I didn't show up, then I would be fired. So, I was fired!

I sat down and talked to Ray's step mom and dad and asked them for advice about work. I didn't want to sponge off of them, but I also didn't want to have them drive me around everywhere. Ray's dad and step mom told me that they would take me to work and back until I got a couple of paychecks to buy a car. Ray's dad found me a car for $500.00 and I was able to be driving myself around again after six weeks. In the mean time, I had quit my college classes for this semester, because I didn't want Ray's step mom to have to drive me to a job and to college classes. I had found a filing job at an insurance company downtown. I hated the job. Filing was so very boring, but there were possibilities of moving up after a few years. I lost the job after six weeks because I was having to take allergy medicine during the Spring allergy season. I kept falling asleep at work. That medicine would just knock me out! My boss called me into her office and told me that she didn't believe that I had what it took to work for them and told me that I was fired. I was very disappointed that I had been fired, but I didn't like the job that much anyway.

I got a job working for Striplings, a nice department store, which wasn't very far from home. I hated the hours though. They wanted me to work nights at least two times a week and I didn't like that because I could never see Ray. I worked there for about two months.

Ray's dad and step mom had been arguing quite a bit lately and I knew that Ray's step mom had been cheating on Ray's dad. She wasn't happy with their marriage because Ray's dad wasn't very romantic. He never took her dancing, so she went without him. She met some man while she was at a Country Western bar and they began having an affair. She had sworn me to secrecy when I found out about it. I didn't want to keep something like this from Ray's dad, but I didn't want to make her angry with me either because I needed a place to live.

Ray's dad wasn't stupid! He realized that something was going on, so he moved out. He moved down to San Antonio. This was scary because he was the person who paid the bills. He told her that he would send some money back to help her raise the kids, but that he needed to find other work and to get away.

A month later, Ray's step mom realized that she really did want to stay married to Ray's dad and she and the kids went down to see him. They were gone for the weekend and when they came back, they told us that they were moving to San Antonio with Ray's dad. They told Ray that we could stay in the house as long as he made the $50.00 per month house payment. We were happy to take the offer because we didn't want to move to San Antonio and we couldn't afford to rent an apartment for $300.00 per month.

Soon as they left, I had to sit down and talk to Ray. I told him that I really didn't want to just live with him. I had SOME morals. I told him that if he planned to marry me, then I would like to know. He said that he would think about it and talk to me about it later.

A few days later, he told me that he had decided. I was very nervous, because he never really showed a strong commitment to marriage before that and I knew that he didn't want to be pushed into one, so I was very unsure about his decision. He told me that he had decided that he DID want to marry me, but that he had already decided that he wanted to wait until October. He set the date for October 21st that year (1978). This was 7 weeks away, but I was glad to hear that he had decided. I began talking about wedding plans, but he quickly told me that he didn't want a big wedding.

As the weeks passed, I was planning a very simple, small wedding and the neighbor lady had agreed to let us use her beautiful back yard. When I told him about the plans, he told me that he didn't want a wedding. He told me that the only thing that he would agree to, was going to the Justice of the

Peace. "YIPPEE! Just what I had always dreamed of," I thought to myself angrily. Oh well, I may as well get used to it. That was just how he was. He didn't like socializing unless partying with drinks and drugs were involved, but surely I could change that after we were married. I just knew that I could get him to change and be the family man that I had always dreamed of.

Just days before our wedding date, I took time to think about what was about to take place. Was this really what I wanted? Was HE really who I wanted? I knew that I wasn't in love, with the type of feelings that I had felt for Kurt, but I thought that maybe they would come later. I knew that I had no where else to go and I would just have to make the best of what I had.

The morning that Ray and I were to be married, I got a phone call. It was my Dad. He called to tell me that he thought that I was making a big mistake but that if this was what I wanted, then I would have to live with it forever. I thanked Dad for his concern, but assured him that I knew what I was doing. I hung up the telephone with tears in my eyes. I didn't want to think about his advice on this particular day. I had made my decision and wanted to make it a happy day. I put the thoughts of the call out of my mind and went on with getting dressed.

We went to the courthouse with a few friends and his cousin Rick and his wife and within a few minutes, we were married. FOR LIFE! TILL DEATH DO US PART! I remembered those words. I was a firm believer in marriage for life, without divorce.

We left our friends for a short honeymoon in San Antonio. His Dad had agreed to pay for a room for us at the San Antonio Inn if we would come down and see them. I was thinking that the name of it sounded really nice and I was glad that we had somewhere to go. Well, I was very surprised to find that it was merely a Truck-stop. We had arrived late that night and before we knew it, it was time to check out. We went to visit his parents and brothers and sister. The were living in an apartment in New Braunfels. We had a short visit and it was time to go home.

I couldn't believe that this was all there was to our marriage and honeymoon. I had been told that a honeymoon would not be very special if you had given yourself away, before you got married. The reality of this had set in. There was nothing to it. Nothing! No special feelings! I would never know what being a TRUE BRIDE would ever be like. I just felt second rate.

Our lives went on from there just like before. He kept having parties with all of his doper friends and I had to live with this. I detested it now. I wanted a better life than this. I was always afraid that we were going to get arrested some day. He had started to sell Marijuana just before I turned 18 and two of us got married! I couldn't believe what he had done. He had bought a whole pound of it and was going to split it up and sell it. I told him that this was Drug Dealing and I didn't like it one bit. He told me that he wouldn't do it for very long, but that he was trying to get ahead on our bills. He even had me help him put it into bags. I didn't want any part of this, but he told me that the faster that it was done, the faster it would be gone. Well, I wanted it gone, so I helped to get it out of our house. After marriage though, he had considered to sell it regularly. I was totally against the idea and firmly let him know my thoughts. After we married, it seemed that my point of view wasn't too important and he continued to sell on a limited basis but tried to keep it away from me.

Ray and his uncle had gotten into a big argument in February and he was fired. His uncle was suspecting that Ray was going to start working for his dad and that they would be in competition with him so he told him to just go on and get lost.

Now what were we going to do? Ray called his dad and told him what had happened, so Ray's dad offered that we move to San Antonio with them for a while. Their plans were to enlarge his tire business so that he could afford to pay Ray. Ray hung up the phone and told me to pack and that we were moving down there.

I was not happy to hear this. I really didn't want to live with his family again. Ray promised me that we wouldn't be there for long but that we had no choice.

We packed our clothing, but left our dishes there. They told us that we could come back for everything in a few weeks.

We had to stay in their two bedroom apartment with their family of 5 and so it was very crowded. The apartment was nice, but too crowded. Ray's step mom started me with her agenda again. I was to help cook and clean up after her kids. I hated living there because the boys were still wetting the bed and this made their room smell really bad. The mattresses were soaked. They would set them out in the sun but they still smelled. Ray's step mom and I started looking for another place to live that would be large enough for all of us. I found out very quickly that this was not a temporary situation. It was going to be a very long one.

We found a large 3 bedroom/2 bath house out in the country on an acre of land. The home was really nice and very large. Ray and I would at least have our own bedroom. It was in Marion, Tx, just a short distance from New Braunfels and San Antonio.

We began going to church with them at the Rock Hills Gospel Church. It was a Spirit-filled, Non-Denominational Church. I still couldn't understand how they could go to church and be Christians and yet they also smoked Marijuana daily.

After being there for four months, I decided that Ray was too content to live there with them, so I decided to get a job. Ray's step mom was against this, because I wouldn't be there to do all the housework again. I was beginning to feel like a Cinderella again. I had to clean up after her children all the time, and I had to put up with their children's rudeness, as well as, be the brunt of the many cruel jokes that they could imagine. I'm not just talking about the kids, it was Ray and Ray's step mom too. Mostly Ray's step mom, but Ray wouldn't do a thing to take up for me. He would just laugh right along with them. It was getting so bad that I was getting overly sensitive. I cried about everything. I was getting to the point that I truly regretted being married to him! I had lost respect for him because he seemed like a loser. I wanted a husband to defend me and to help us make it on our own.

I found a job at a Navy Recruiting Office. I would be a secretary. It was a very nice job in a very small office. My job was to file papers, send mail outs and type up Recruit Testing paper work. I was determined that we would move out of their house in six weeks!

Several high school boys and other men, came into the office to inquire about possible recruitment. One young man even came in just to visit because he was on leave for a month. This young man was very cute and started visiting the office daily. He always stayed and talked to me for a while and he became a good friend. He asked me about my marriage and I told him that I was miserably trying to live with a poor decision, till death do we part. I told him that I often thought that dying would be alot better than facing their ridicule all the time. He couldn't believe that my husband would allow this to go on. It really made me feel better to talk to another guy about this. It helped me to check my perspective and to see that I wasn't being unrealistic in my expectations of a husband. This guy sent me roses the next day and the note read that he hoped that the flowers would brighten my day since things were going so badly for me. How Sweet!!! He kept coming by and would always compliment me and tell me that my husband just didn't know how to appreciate such a beautiful wife. He even took me out to lunch, you know, just a friendly lunch. We had become very good friends in the three weeks that he had been home and it was almost time for him to return. I was really attached to him and told him that I didn't know how I would ever make it without him. He was my total encouragement! He told me that I was more than welcomed to come with him to California to live with him. Oh how tempting! I told him that I couldn't do that because I was married. He insisted that what I had was no marriage and that he could definitely make me happier!

That evening, I went home very confused. Did I really have a marriage?

Another evening of ridicule occurred and the next day, I went to visit this Navy guy and to ask him if his offer was serious. He seemed hesitant but told me that I could come with him. He warned me that this was not a commitment or anything, but that we could see how things would go.

I went home and began packing my things. I had decided that there had to be a better life than what I had there and I may as well try to find it. Ray came home and found me packing my things. He looked at me and asked me what I was doing? I told him that I could no longer be his doormat nor tolerate being "the family joke". I told him that I was leaving! He asked me where I was going and I just told him that I had found another place to live. Then he laid on the bed and watched me pack. He didn't say a word. When I had put the last of my things into my suitcase, I turned and asked him curtly, "So you have nothing to say? Not even good-bye?" He asked me what he was supposed to say. I told him that he could at least say that he was sorry for what he had allowed to happen. I then told him that I had married him to be his wife forever, but I felt that he didn't care about our marriage and I was finished. He said good-bye and as I grabbed my things, he softly spoke up and said, "Can I ask you something?" I said, "Of course." He asked, "What can I say to get you to change your mind?" I started crying and told him that he could assure me that he loved me enough to never allow them to run me down again. I also asked that he move us out of his parents home. He reached out to touch my hand, as he had never done before. He actually had a look of love for me that I had never seen before and he had tears running down his face. He told me that he was sorry that he had not been a better husband, but that he would try if I would stay. That was all I ever needed to hear!

We did move out a few weeks later and got an apartment in town. We always had to have a room mate to help us to afford our rent and Ray even got another job to earn a real paycheck, working construction. Our marriage was getting much better! We were going to church still and he wasn't smoking pot anymore! I was very happy that I had decided to stay!

Five months after we had moved out we were about to celebrate our anniversary. We went out to dinner with our friend and my co-worker from the Navy Office - Greg to celebrate. I was nervous and excited about this dinner though, because I had something to tell Ray and I didn't know how to tell him.

After our drinks were brought to the table (iced tea), Greg said that he would like to make an anniversary toast to us. After he had made the toast, he asked if he could move into our second bedroom, since we had lost our other room mates. Ray spoke up and said that he liked the idea and then Greg turned to ask me. I thought that this would be the moment to let the news out because Greg might not want to live in the apartment with us because I was pregnant. My reply was, "I guess that it would be OK with me as long as you could stand to live in the house with a pregnant woman." They both nearly choked on their drink! "Pregnant?!" they both asked? I nodded yes and looked at Ray to tell him that I didn't know how to tell him. I was worried that he would be angry because he had already told me that he wanted us to wait a year before we started to try.

He was smiling. Greg asked him if he was happy and he told him that he was. He said that he was going to be a father and that he was really glad!

He and Greg went to the apartment after dinner and started celebrating by drinking. I went on to bed because I was very tired. I was glad to know that Ray was happy about the news and just hoped that he would continue to change for the better. Ray wound up getting very drunk that night and blacked out. Greg woke me to tell me that he was worried about Ray and that he wanted me to help him get Ray into bed. While we were trying to get him into bed, he awoke! He started screaming and fighting and it was apparent that he didn't know where he was. He had pushed me so hard that I hit the wall, so Greg pinned him down to keep him from injuring me. He was able to get Ray to understand where he was and get himself oriented. Then, he went to sleep for the night.

His parents weren't happy about the news at all! Ray's step mom even suggested ways to cause a miscarriage. They didn't think that we were ready to have children. Well, it didn't matter if we were ready or not, the fact was, that we WERE having a baby.

Ray continued to stay away from the Marijuana, but still drank some. When I was 4 months pregnant, we had to move out of our apartment because Greg had been reassigned and moved away and the management had raised the cost of our rent. We were going to have to start paying for doctor bills and we knew that we wouldn't be able to pay higher rent. We found a little 8' x 30' trailer for rent nearby and had to move into it because we were both determined that we couldn't live with his family again. This little trailer was just a travel trailer. It was only large enough to have our bed in it, and no room for anything else. There was no heat there, except for the oven. The cooking oven! The gas was so strong in the oven, that I was afraid to go to sleep for fear that I would never wake up. We were there for a month, when Ray's dad had received a call from his brother, asking if Ray would come back up there and go to work for him. Ray's dad told us about the offer and we were quick to accept. We moved the next day!

Chapter 9: Life in full circle

We found a little duplex for rent near Vickery street in Ft. Worth and it wasn't very far from his work. It was small, but SO much larger than the little trailer. It was also warm!

I decided to try to call my Dad and Mom to see if they would consider reconciling. When I called, Mom answered the phone and I asked to speak to Dad. I told her that I knew that they were still angry with me, but that I just wanted to apologize and tell them some news! Dad took the telephone and I asked him if he would ever consider forgiving me? He said that he just didn't know if he was ready or not and then I told him that I was pregnant and that he was going to be a Grandfather. He wasn't thrilled with the news, but I told him that Ray and I had made several changes and that we were going to church now. He was glad to hear that and he said that I could call again sometime. A few weeks later, I called again and asked if we could visit. They accepted and invited us to dinner.

Ray wasn't thrilled about this because he didn't like knowing that they didn't approve of him. At least he finally agreed to go over there with me. Things quickly fell back into place and our relationship was mended with them!

Things went well for about a month, but Ray started going out drinking with old friends again and smoking marijuana with them again. We only went to church once or twice and he lost interest after that.

One night, he went out to play pool with his single male friends. He was spending all of his spare time with, and this time he was gone until after 11:00 pm. I decided that I had put up with this too long, so I drove to the place where I knew he would be and walked in and surprised him! A friend of our knew of the local bar that they were playing at. After she told me, I drove straight over there and I walked up to him and asked him to step outside with me. He laughed at me at first because he was already intoxicated somewhat. He saw that I was very serious and so he went outside with me and that is when I gave him an ultimatum. I told him that he could decide, right then and there, who he chose to be married to. His single friends or his pregnant wife? I told him that if he didn't come with me right then, then I was gone forever ! He looked at me for a moment and started to say something stupid, but told me that he would go with me! I was stunned! He was so worried about being bossed around by a wife that I thought, for sure, that he would tell me to get lost! At least he stopped hanging out with these loser friends and started staying home more. The time was near that I was about to deliver. I was due in May 1980 and this was already April! I had taken a temporary job at John Peter Smith Hospital in the Medical Records office. It was a contract job, so they understood that I may have to quit after only working a few weeks, but this was OK with them. By being employed there, it helped us out on the cost of having our baby there. We were already on a reduced rate plan and Ray even gave blood a few times to make a payment.

My contract ended on May 1st and they wouldn't renew it again because I was due any day. At least we thought that it was any day. I later found out that the doctor in New Braunfels was wrong about my due date and that I wasn't due until May 26th instead of the 14th. I was so depressed. I missed Mother's Day! The 26th had come and almost gone, but at 10:00pm that night, I went into labor. We stayed up for an hour waiting to see if it was the real thing and when the contractions had been steadily coming 5 minutes apart, we decided to go to the hospital.

Mom came up to the hospital to sit with Ray and be there to wait. I was actually very happy that she was there and even hoped that this would be a new beginning for everyone.

Twenty one hours later, I delivered a boy. Ray was so glad that we had a boy that he impulsively decided to make a change in the name that we had chosen. We had decided to call him Aaron William , because of a message that was delivered to me by a lady in a church meeting. When she approached me at the meeting, she asked me if I would obey the Lord in my choice of names for my child. "Well of course I would," I told her, "if I knew that the Lord was telling me to do this!" Then she said something chilling, "The Lord has told me that you were very concerned about your child's health but He wants you to know that "HE" has all 10 fingers and all 10 toes. The Lord would have you to name your first-born son Aaron!" I quickly asked her if the Lord was trying to tell me that this was a boy, but she said that she could only tell me the very words that the Lord had told her to deliver to me. She said that this was all that the Lord had told her to tell me. WOW! I felt chill bumps all over! I really felt that she had heard from the Lord because I had never told anyone that I was worried that my child would be deformed! One problem though! I was really wanting a girl! BUT! I was willing to accept the Lord's will for me and if having a boy was his will, then so be it!

Ray came into the recovery room just glowing! He had already seen his son at the window. The nurses had even let Ray see him at the door just before they bathed him and began weighing and measuring. He asked me if we could call him Randall (a name similar to his real name)? I told him that I wanted to do as the Lord had asked and call him Aaron and so he suggested Randall Aaron. I just couldn't tell him No! I hoped that the Lord wouldn't mind it that Aaron was his middle name.

It was the next day before I ever got to hold my baby. In county hospitals, you don't receive many services. You are basically treated like a heard of cattle. When I got a room, the nurses brought my baby in to feed him. This was the first time that I had held him and I really didn't get to see him very clearly in the delivery room because they told me to inhale some gas so that I could endure the pain while being repaired from delivery. I didn't realize that the gas causes very blurry vision!

Here I was. All alone in my room with my very own baby. I held him and looked at him all over. I checked his diaper to see if he was dirty and then a nurse came in to talk to me about breast feeding. I had decided that I wanted to give it a try. I didn't feel very comfortable with the idea, but Ray asked me to try it! He told me that it would be less expensive for us.

The nurse tried to help me out, but I just didn't like it and the baby didn't seem to either. He just cried. I tried for two days and couldn't get comfortable with the idea, so I changed my mind and told them that I was going to bottle feed. I was very nervous every time I held the baby. It felt very strange.

Mom came to the hospital to take us home, because Ray had to work. She even came in and cleaned up the house for me when we walked in and found it a mess! I was hurting very badly and needed to lie down. While I was resting, she helped to clean up the house. She was not happy to find that Ray left it such a mess for us to come home to. I later found out that he had gone out and gotten drunk and that was why the plants had been knocked over on the floor and the sheet was hanging outside. I didn't want Mom to know though.

That first night was a real eye-opener as to what life was going to be like from now on. The baby had taken a nap that afternoon for about three hours and now, at 2:00 am he was determined to never go back to sleep. I was feeling miserable and had asked Ray to help me at 3:00 am. I was trying to let Ray sleep since he had to work the next morning, but by this time, I was exhausted and crying. I didn't know what to do to get this baby back to sleep. Didn't he understand that I was tired?

At 3:45 am, we had called Ray's step mom and asked her what to do. Ray's step mom and dad had come to town to see us and were staying a Troy and Della's. (Ray's grandfather and step grandmother). Ray's step mom told us to pack up the baby's bottles and diapers and she would come and pick us all up and she would sit up with the baby so that we could get some sleep. I was happy about this, because I was not doing a very good job and could certainly learn from someone else about how to handle a baby!

I eventually got the hang of it and tried to be the very best mother. I taught my baby everything I could. I stayed at home with him to be a real mother.

My mother got the news that I had a new baby and she called me and asked me if she could come and visit. She rode the bus into town and stayed with us for a week.

While she was there, she told us that she had remarried again to a man named Tom. She said that they had both recently quit drinking and that they were both helping to counsel other alcoholics. I was very happy for her. Our visit was nice and at the end of the week, she returned home.

Two weeks later, we got a call from her asking us if she could come and live with us for a while because Tom had started drinking again. We reluctantly told her that she could. She stayed with us for six weeks before she found a job as a live in nurse to an elderly woman in the area.

We had moved from our little duplex into a two bedroom house when Randall was six weeks old. The landlord of the duplex told us that she just couldn't put up with the baby crying so much. He only cried at nights but it was every single night. He never wanted to sleep, so I finally took some advice to let him cry himself to sleep so that he would tire out and go to sleep. He cried for 45 minutes straight every night at 11:00 until 11:45 pm. He was just like a time clock. We knew that by midnight, he would stop and be asleep.

The new two bedroom house was on the north side of town, not too far from Ray's grandparent's house. Della was a big help with Randall. She loved babies and we visited often. It wasn't much longer before Ray's step mom and dad moved back to Ft. Worth, not too far from us, because they wanted to be near their grandson.

Randall was a perfect child, except for the sleeping problem. He slept through the night at a week old. He was crawling at five months old, weaned from the bottle at 7 months old and eating table food, walking at 9 months old and POTTY trained at 9 1/2 months. Yes! potty trained. He never even had an accident. I felt that I was a very good mother because I knew children that were 4 years old that still wore diapers. Randall was just one of those babies who liked to please people. He meticulously cleaned up his toys and placed them on the shelf just like I would. I always thought that he was a very smart child, but I also thought that I must be a good mother to have such an easy time of raising a baby that was so good. When Randall was 10 months old, I found out that I was pregnant again. When I realized that raising babies was so easy, I decided that I wanted to have another one now. I wanted to have two children. A boy and a girl. I wanted to finish having children at a young age so that I could be young with my children as they grew. Afterwards, when I was old, they would be gone!

Ray wasn't real excited about having another so soon, but he told me that he would consent since everything was going OK. (At least things were going well now.) When Randall was just 6 months old, Ray had tried to kill me because I went to get him out of another bar. He was hanging out with single friends again and staying at the pool halls drinking. I decided to try the ultimatum again, since it had worked previously. This time, I had to take Randall in the car with me to the bar, and when I went in, I found him drunk with his friends. This time, he did not leave with me! He did come home about 30 minutes later and he told me that I had better never threaten to leave with his son again and he grabbed me by the throat and pinned me against the wall and started choking me. I thought that he was going to kill me. I saw a very evil look in his eyes and when I started crying, and choking for a breath of air, he realized that he was really killing me and he stopped. He looked at his hands and starting crying and saying that he was sorry, but I was so terrified that I ran out of the house and went to a neighbor's house to call his parents.

Ray realized that night, that he was having some serious drinking problems.

He had asked his Dad to pray for him that he would never touch the stuff again. He begged for my forgiveness and promised me that he would never drink again. He also promised that we would start going to church again! I hoped that he was sincere.

The very next Sunday, we were in church. We went to the Living Word Center Church. This was where his Dad had gone before he moved to San Antonio and we had visited a few times before. The Pastor's name was Pastor Stan. I loved this church. The message of Christ was one of such a loving, merciful God. We went faithfully for about four months and then Ray started missing here and there. By the time that I was eight months pregnant, he was rarely going at all. I finally had to decide if I was going to serve the Lord in spite of the fact that Ray may never be faithful. My walk with God was strictly between God and me, not Ray, God and me. I had a very difficult time learning to go to church without him, but I learned.

November 30th, I had another baby boy. Something very strange had happened to me the moment that they handed me my baby (which was within seconds after delivery). I held him and began crying. I had a feeling come over me as though a ton of bricks were being removed from around my heart. I was experiencing the feeling of real love for the very first time. I had never felt this kind of emotional energy. I held him so tightly and enjoyed every moment! I just kept crying so hard, but not from pain, from joy. A joy and feeling of love that I had never experienced. I realized immediately, that my heart had just been freed from the bondage of my past. When I was a child, it was never permitted that anyone ever hold me or cuddled me, or give affection to me. I never knew what affection felt like. This is obviously what it meant for a Mother to bond with her baby. I kept thanking God for these feelings. The nurses had to insist to take my baby to clean him and weigh him. I told them that I wanted him back just the moment that they were finished. I waited anxiously for the chance to hold him again. When they brought him back, I held him again, and still felt that deep, warm feeling of love. I could only thank God over and over for this double blessing! I realized that this type of bond had never occurred with Randall. I was concerned about this lack in our relationship, but thought the bond would be there with Randall as well, since I had been given this new sense of love that night. I felt that everything in my life would change now.

We named this baby, Joel William . The Lord had given me a dream when I conceived him that I had two boys and that their names were Aaron and Joel. I had talked to Ray's dad about the dream and he told me that he had also had a dream that I was having another boy named Joel. I knew very deeply that God was telling me to name him Joel. When the Lord gives you a dream, it is very different from an ordinary dream!

The Lord was continuing to teach me many things. I learned that I didn't have to have my past, cripple my future. I enjoyed being a Mother. It didn't seem as mechanical as it was the first time. Experience had a little bit to do with this, but not much, because Joel was a totally different baby than Randall was. He was very good at sleeping but that was about it! As he grew older, we found him to be a total opposite from Randall. We had nicknamed Randall - "Mr. Clean" because he was such a perfectionist at picking up his toys and pretending to vacuum and to even help wipe up messes for me. Joel, on the other hand, earned the nickname - "Messy Marvin" because he made one mess after another and could have cared less if anything was ever clean. By the way, he wasn't potty-trained at 9 months old either. I was counting my blessings to have him trained before the next child arrived.

Ray was falling back into the rut of spending very little time at home. He took up a new sport - golf. I hated the fact that he would get off of work early Saturdays and spend the rest of the afternoon and until dark at the golf course. He rarely spent time with us. Our marriage had fallen into a big rut. I filled my time with my children and learned to feel fulfillment from them because he just didn't care.

The Lord intervened though. When Joel was five months old, Ray came in from work late and told me that something had happened that he knew was a "Warning Sign" from God. The police had pulled him over when the officer spotted him actually driving and smoking Marijuana. He knew that he was going to jail, but the Officer got an emergency call and had to respond. The officer ran off telling him that this was his "lucky day!" He confessed to me that he had been taking pills and smoking marijuana for a few months and was even selling these, to support his habit, so that I wouldn't be suspicious of the missing money.

I was just thankful that I hadn't known that he was doing these things because I would have fallen apart. I had two babies to worry about and just couldn't have dealt with that stress too!

Ray started going to church again and was fairly faithful for several months. Sometimes, he would go and golf instead of going with us, but at least he was going occasionally.

When Joel was 15 months old, I had another strange dream. It was another dream that I felt was from the Lord, but hoped that I was wrong this time. I dreamed that I was going to have a baby girl. When I woke up, I was sweating. I certainly hoped that the dream was wrong, because I had changed my mind about wanting any more children. Joel had been a handful and the two of them together got into all sorts of things. How could these two little babies get into so much? I was constantly busy with them. It was very expensive too. Joel wasn't potty trained and nearly broken from the bottle now and I was dreaming about another child!

The dream was true. I found out that I was pregnant just a few weeks after that dream. Ray was devastated! He was even angry and accused me of not being careful enough. We both had cried for quite a while and then he left the house. He told me that he needed to go think. I was worried that he was going to drink, or even worse! I had called some friends from church to come over and pray for us and afterward, Ray came home. He said that he knew that things couldn't be changed and he would just have to accept this and carry on. Our only consolation was the dream! The dream had shown that I was going to have a baby girl.

The dream was true. Nine months later, our little girl was born, the little girl that I had dreamed of having since I was 9 years old. We were all elated! A girl seemed to be such a blessing to all of us! We named her Rachel Ranae. I had looked through the names in the Bible for a name that would be fitting. The name Rachel meant, "sheep like." I took that to mean, "very calm". That's was just what I needed! A very calm child because these boys were wild! Ranae was my middle name and I thought that it sounded nice with Rachel.

It was so much fun to dress her in pretty little clothes. I made her several little outfits and had fixed her room up with everything that I had made myself. The room was all done in purple and white, with matching curtains. It looked frilly!

We had moved into a brand new Mobile Home just after we found out that I was pregnant because the little house was crowded already. Our mobile home was on a rented lot in Haltom City right near Watauga. It was a very beautiful mobile home. We seemed to be very blessed.

We had started a little janitorial business that was helping us to have a little more income. Our plans were, to make the janitorial business large enough so that Ray could quit working with his uncle. He hated coming in with tire dirt on him every day and sweating in the hot sun all the time. When we started the business, Ray told me that he wanted this business to be blessed by God and he was going to try to use it to help others. He even gave the business a Christian name.

It was very evident that the Lord had blessed this business. We knew nothing about what we were doing when we first began, and we were getting accounts that we should have never been awarded. We saw the Lord open doors left and right. Within the very first year, he was able to quit working for his uncle and even hired some help. Our business grew faster than we had ever imagined. God had given me the gift to meet people and influence them towards our business. I took care of the bookkeeping and eventually, the business grew to the point where we had to get an office space to work from. We had to hire several part time employees to handle all the work.

Ray worked nights, on one of the cleaning routes, and I did all the other work. We were good at this and our talents complimented each other nicely.

When Rachel was three years old, we were blessed with a new home. This home was very large. It was more than I had ever dreamed of living in! We were driving new cars now and had nice furniture. It was very apparent that our labors had been blessed.

A year or two after we had moved in, I found out that Ray was beginning to drink again. He even drank with two new members of the church, who were now working for us. I was appalled! I was scared too! I hoped that his old lifestyle had not crept back in. I pleaded with him to stop, but he told me that a drink now and then wouldn't hurt him. He basically let me know that he would do what ever he wanted to do. I could only pray for God to deal with him because I had already learned that I couldn't change him.

In 1988, I had been adventuresome. I went out to ride on a Civilian Ride

Program with a Grand Prairie Police Officer. I thought that it would be a lot of fun, and I thoroughly enjoyed it. The officers had told me about the Police Reserve program, which was a program in which people trained for through the police academy, and then volunteered their services as police officers for that city. They told me that the city would pay for the training and even the uniform. I was very intrigued!

I went home and ran the idea past Ray. He had already mentioned that I should have something to do, outside of the home, so that I could have a break from the kids. This was what I wanted to do! That is, as long as he didn't mind. I always felt that he was the leader of the home and I would never go against his will. When I asked him about it, he told me to do whatever I wanted to do. He didn't act like he cared one way or the other, so I checked into the details. I found out that they would be testing for Reserve Officer positions soon and I placed my name on the list. Within a couple of weeks, I was notified of the testing dates. The tests consisted of a written test and a physical agility test. I had two weeks to prepare. I prayed first that I would be in God's will and I asked the Lord to help me to pass the test, ONLY if it WAS his will. I had also asked God to confirm his will by having Ray actually tell me that I had his blessings on this. I didn't want to do anything to hurt our marriage because we were happy now, in spite of his occasional drinking. I just wanted something to make me feel more secure. If anything ever happened to Ray and I was left to care for three children alone, then I would need some type of training to fall back on. It seemed like a very sensible idea. I also felt that it would be a wonderful way to help others!

Well, after a bit of confusion, I got Ray's words of blessings to go to take the test. I passed! It wasn't an easy test. I also had to pass the background checks and a Review Board before being accepted. I passed these too. By October 1988, I was in the Police Academy.

Chapter 10: My own identity!?!

The Police Academy was going to take 6 months to complete. Classes were four evenings a week and all day Saturdays. This was going to be a big change for our home because Ray had never taken care of the children on a regular basis before. He told me that he didn't mind doing this and he thought that I needed to do this for myself. I was so surprised that he was doing this for me. I literally gained a new respect for him and for our marriage!

It was very different for me to be gone so much, but my determination to achieve helped me to be tough. I did business work during the day, and tried to have dinner cooked before I would leave at night. It was tough to juggle my chores as a mother, my duties to our business, school and even home-work, but somehow I managed to keep things running smoothly. Ray was doing a good job with the kids too. They enjoyed spending time with him. Before this, they rarely spent time together because he was always working, or playing softball, or golfing, but rarely just spending time with them.

A few weeks after I had begun the Academy, our 10th Anniversary came up. I had planned a very special weekend for us and I just knew that he would love it. It was all a little rendezvous that was a big surprise. I hoped that this would prove to him how much I loved him and how much I appreciated his support. We had not been very close in a sexual way because of some old scars of mine and some bad habits of his and it was just beginning to get better, so this weekend should really be special!

The weekend was very successful and he told me afterward that it had been the best time of his life. He loved every little plan that I had made and wasn't upset about the cost. He said that it had been worth every penny. For me, it had seemed like the honeymoon that we had never had. It was a great boost for our marriage.

By the fourth month of the Police Academy, I could see that Ray was ready for me to be finished. I felt that he may not have realized how long 6 months really took. He was beginning to seem more impatient with me. I promised him that it would all be over soon and that I would be forever grateful.

When the Academy classes were finished, I graduated second in the class! This was the first thing that I had ever done that made me feel so successful.

I had been a mother and a good business woman, but there was something different about reaching this goal. It was not that I felt independent from my husband, but my fears of being left alone without any skills, were gone. I now had the training necessary to get a job if the need arose. I felt like a success, even though I knew that the Lord had made me successful. I thanked my family for their support and told Ray that he had proven his love for me by helping me to achieve this goal. It had seemed to make up for all the bad scenes of our past.

When I graduated from the Academy, April 30, 1989, I had to fulfill the minimum volunteer requirements of serving 16 hours a month for the Grand Prairie Police Department. At first, that was about all that I would do. I went on Friday nights for about 4 - 6 hours and worked in the Jail, until I could get a Field Training Officer assigned to me to train me for the actual street work.

We had begun to suffer in our business this year and we were struggling a little, financially. I continued to try to get new accounts to cover the ones that we were losing. We had watched the Lord do one miracle after another for 5 years. Now we weren't seeing many miracles at all. Ray was now rarely attending church and I felt that his commitment to the Lord was changing. He started telling me to cut back on our tithes to the church, and was drinking more now than he had been. I knew that the business stresses were bothering him, but these choices were not the right answers.

In the first quarter of 1990, we had lost 75% of our business. It was a very bad year for the nation's economy and businesses were having to cut back. It seemed like the Janitorial Services were the first place to make cuts. Business either accepted such low bids from other services that we could not compete with, or began doing the work themselves. Either way, we lost their contracts. Ray kept telling me to go out and get more business, but everywhere I turned, the doors closed. It was as though God had taken all the blessings away that he had given to us. I kept telling Ray that it was because of his promise to God. He told the Lord that he would be faithful to him if he would bless the business. God kept his promise, but Ray had not.

I finished my Field Training at the Police Department and began working there a couple of days a week. I felt that I needed to work and actually use my new skills so that I would feel proficient and comfortable. I was nervous at first because everything was so new. The best training for me was to actually do the work! I didn't think that I was doing any harm, because I was gone while the kids were in school. I worked on Friday nights also because that was the busiest time when I could learn the most. I really liked police work.

Since our business was going under, Ray decided that maybe it was time for him to try another career also. He went into Real Estate school. He did very well and in just a few months, he was ready to take his final state exam. He studied for hours and days. He told me that it was really hard for him to remember all of the math formulas. Time came for the exam and he failed it. He told me that he had dropped his calculator during the exam and there was no way that he could have finished the test without it. This calculator had special functions that were essential to working the calculations that were on the test. He was sure that he had failed. He got his test results and found that he was right. I encouraged him to take it over as soon as possible. He told me that he was finished. He seemed to have lost his courage.

He started drinking more heavily after this. We weren't getting along very well either. He spent his time at the softball fields, where he knew that he could drink, and I spent my three times per week at the police department.

The business had brought us some very close friends and had also destroyed a few friendships along the way. We had some tough business decisions to make and since we were working with several of our friends, we were certain to go through these difficulties. As long as we were serving the Lord, we seemed to make the right decisions. We found that there were a few friends that got jealous or became greedy.

Some of our very best friends were Andy and Cathy. The little bit of socializing we did, was usually with them. Since they were so involved with our business, and had even begun their own business after they learned the ropes, we just seemed to always find ourselves together. We also went to the same church and played softball together on the church league. Ray and Andy were the Ladies' Team Coaches. Cathy and I enjoyed having them with us as coaches. They were good at softball and almost led us to a big victory. We only lost the season by 1 game.

Ray and Andy had begun playing softball at other places, outside of the church league and this is really when they began drinking. A beer or two during or after a game was common among the ball players, but these two men were playing with a time bomb. Both were candidates to become alcoholics.

Andy even began having a long time affair with one of our closest friends and his marriage to Cathy was eventually destroyed by it. Cathy had tried to forgive him and they went to counseling, but his need for attention from other women was stronger than his love for Cathy. Shortly after their divorce, Cathy asked a few of her friends to go to the coast with her. She asked me and Sue (one of our other closest friends) and Sharon. Sharon was a mother of four children and her husband had worked for us for a long time. None of us had ever been on a vacation without our husbands and I didn't even want to, but I also knew that Cathy needed us and this is what she thought would help her get over the divorce.

I asked Ray if he would mind if I went along with them and he consented. I could tell that he wasn't real happy about it, but he wasn't going to say no.

We all piled into my car and headed to Galveston. We stayed at the Flagship Inn right over the water. It was beautiful. Ray and I had been there with Cathy and Andy just a year or two before. That had been our first vacation since we had been married. He made me angry by cutting our first vacation a day short, so that he could get back to work. We had planned to be gone for only three and half days.

While we were there, we checked out the beaches that first night and since it was so late, we went on to bed. We shopped, went swimming in the ocean and in the pool at the hotel, and then went out for dinner and walked around town. It was still fairly early, so we decided to check out the hotel's night club. Sue and I stayed in the night club to listen to the musicians for a while, but Sharon and Cathy went back up to their room. They were in a strange mood. Later, Sue and I went up to see if they were alright. Sharon was on the telephone and she was crying. Her husband, Sam, was giving her a big guilt trip about being away without him and she decided that she wanted to go home. Cathy told Sue and I that she wasn't having any fun either. She had hoped to come and celebrate her divorce and forget things for a while, but she found out that a divorce was nothing to celebrate. She said that she could only feel sick over it and just wanted to go home. Sue and I didn't want to go back yet With such a long drive down there, we didn't want to just turn around and drive back. Sharon and Cathy packed up and had the hotel shuttle take them to the airport and they went home that night. Since I had to drive home, I wanted to wait until the next day to drive home.

Sue and I went back down to the lounge to see what was going on. The musicians were playing some really good music that Sue and I really liked. We were asked to dance a few times and we also met another couple there from Dallas. When we began talking, we found out that we had alot in common. Her husband was a cop! We started talking about some police things then and wound up staying up late talking about all sorts of things. We had danced a few more dances with some men that had asked us and before we knew it, it was 2:00 am. Sue had gone out to the car for something and struck up a conversation with the security guard. I sat and talked to the younger guy that I had danced with a few times. This guy was several years younger than I was, but he hung around me like I was his same age. We talked about all sorts of things and we went walking. We were only walking down the pier, so I didn't see any harm in that. Then, we started looking for Sue and the Security Guard. I couldn't get into the room until I found Sue because she had our key. I didn't find her until 4:30 am. I had been talking to this guy all that time, and when we were saying good-bye, he leaned over and kissed me goodnight. I felt so guilty! I was a married woman, and this young man just kissed me! I went to bed and cried about how I had been so stupid to let him kiss me. Sure, he had caught me off guard, but I felt guilty that I had let him feel that it was OK to try. I had such a guilty conscience. When Sue and I woke up, I was ready to go home, but Sue wasn't yet. We had made a deal to wait until noon to leave. When we got home, I was still overcome with guilt. I couldn't even face Ray because I felt so bad about the situation. I had wished that I had never gone.

There WAS one good point about the trip. I had met that Dallas Police Officer and he had given me his home number and told me to call him when we got home and he would arrange for me to go out and ride with him and his partner. I was really anxious to ride out with them because of the type of beat that they worked in. It was one of the roughest in Dallas. I really wanted to see what this would be like, so I called him and made arrangements to ride that next week.

When Ray found out that I was going to the Dallas PD to ride with another officer, he began asking all sorts of questions. I told him that Sue and I had met him and his wife at Galveston and that he had simply offered for me to ride out. Ray told me that he didn't like the idea but didn't tell me that I could not go. I wasn't trying to hide anything or I wouldn't have told him the plans to go.

While we had only been out on the streets for a little over an hour, Ray paged me. I called him right back and he told me that I would regret my decision. I didn't understand why he was upset with me. I asked the officers if they would stop by my mother-in-law's house to see if I could call home. They weren't too far away, so they stopped by. We all went inside and I introduced the officers to his mother. After we spoke for a minute, and I called home but no one answered so we left. I had a very bad feeling about this and asked the officers to take me back to the station so that I could go home. They took me after they got a break from their calls and I called home again and found that no one was home. I went back over to his mother's house and found Ray and the kids there. I approached Ray and asked him what was going on and he snapped at me sharply that I could just go home and leave them all alone. He began accusing me of having an affair with the officer. I couldn't believe that he had thought this. I would never have an affair! I began crying and trying to explain that I wasn't trying to run around on him and that I didn't want our marriage to break up. He just ordered me to get out of his face before he slapped me and so I walked off for a moment. I went in and tried to talk to his mother. I tried to get her to reason with him. She would only say that she thought that Ray was pretty serious about leaving me and that he had asked her if he and the kids could move in. I couldn't believe it! How could he do this?

I went back outside and demanded that we go and talk alone because I was not about to let our marriage end over a misunderstanding like this. He finally agreed to go and talk. I had told him that I would never have an affair with anyone. I even confessed to him how guilty I felt for my stupidity in allowing a guy to kiss me. He nearly exploded over that. He told me that he had known that something went on in Galveston, but he wasn't sure what had happened. He said that he had a feeling deep inside, that I was doing something wrong. I explained to him that this kiss wasn't something that I was expecting and that I was not trying to have any affair. He saw that I was very sincere and so he forgave me for my stupidity. We went back and picked up the kids and went home. This was not the end of our troubles. Troubles were just beginning!

Chapter 11: The end results

Things were going along fine for a few weeks but not for long. I was at work one Friday night at the police department and Cathy had paged me to tell me that Ray had just dropped her drunken husband out from a cab at their house and that Ray was walking home. She told me that they had been out drinking for several hours and they were too drunk to drive home so they got a cab. Andy had passed out in the cab on their way to Andy's house. Ray was barely sober enough to drag Andy out of the cab and into his house. Ray was going to walk home but Cathy thought that he was in no shape to make it. It was 1:30 am and I was worried that he would get caught by Watauga Police if her were found walking the streets in a drunken state, so I tried to call a friend from church to see if he would find him for me. It would take me 40 minutes to get home and I knew that he could be in jail by then. Our close friend, Tim lived only a few blocks away, so he went to find him.

I left work and hurried home. Tim told me that he had looked everywhere and couldn't find him. While we were talking, Ray walked in. He was really drunk. I was so angry at him, but I kept my mouth shut that night. I just wanted to get him to bed.

I had started making close friends with the other officers at work and I finally started talking to a couple of them about Ray. I was only asking other men's opinions about my reactions or overreactions to things that were going on at home. Dave's opinions of my situations really caught my attention. Dave was a single man that had been divorced for quite some time. We became very close friends. He always knew how to make me laugh and he certainly made me feel good because he was continually complimenting me. He told me that he couldn't believe that my husband didn't appreciate me and that Ray was acting like an irresponsible jerk. I listened and absorbed all of his nice things that he had to say about me and felt that he was very complimentary.

Ray began making several poor choices with respect to alcohol and his activities that took him away from us. Finally, I got to the point where I just didn't care if he knew where I was or not. I was trying to teach him a lesson. When I was asked by the other guys if I wanted to go out to a club one night, I decided to go. I asked myself. "Why not?" Let him see what it's like to have the shoe on the other foot. I went out with them to some night club to dance. I was dancing with a guy from work and he was really cute. He told me numerous times how good I looked and that caused me to fall right into the trap. I was sunk. I fell into a state of sin, that night, that I never thought that I was capable of. I actually loved receiving compliments that I looked good or looked hot! I wasn't used to hearing this at all. My goals were definitely turned away from trying to be a good Christian mother, to wanting more and more attention from men. I loved to hear that I looked nice. I felt good about myself for a change. I had realized that I was actually pretty. Ever since I had started the Police Academy, I was always receiving compliments and even embarrassing gestures from men. I was so embarrassed by them, but yet flattered.

I was wearing more daring clothes than ever before and always trying to look my best. I wanted to look sexy and I knew that if I looked really good when I was around the guys at work, that I would get more compliments. My ego was being totally fed by other men and none at all from my own husband. I had really wanted his attention, but when he only gave me put-downs, I became disheartened. I learned that my ego needed to be constantly filled. The bigger it became, the more attention I needed. I had taken my eyes off of the most important part of my life and that was my relationship with the Lord. I still went to church, but my relationship with God was deteriorating.

From the time that I married Ray and up to the time where I went to Galveston with my girlfriends, I had only ONE goal in my life and that goal was to be a wife and a mother and to be the best Police Officer that I could ever be. I sought help from God to be able to achieve these goals. I was a faithful wife who was never even interested in looking at a photo of a nice looking man. My friends would think that I was crazy when I wouldn't drool over a beautiful, manly specimen passing by us. I really had no desires outside of my marriage, IN SPITE of the fact, that our marriage was so one-sided for the first 9 years of being married. I hated sex! I felt that sex was merely a wifely duty to keep from losing your husband. Sometimes sex was convenient though, especially if I wanted Ray to allow me to go shopping. I never felt that I was receiving affection from him. He only showed affection when he was in need. He also continuously put me down by saying that I was either too fat or too saggy! (I was never more than 15 pounds over weight and that was after having our third child.) Our interests were totally different except for the success of our business. My friends couldn't possibly understand why I didn't ever want to go on any trips without my husband. But, my only pleasures in life were to please the Lord - #1, to please my husband - #2, be a good mother - #3, and to serve other people - #4! Life was totally complete like this.

Becoming a Police Officer was only a fulfillment of #4 until I lost sight of my other goals.

It was as though I had sipped from a cup of poison. The compliments that I was receiving outside of my home, had begun to cause an insatiable desire to hear more. I had been starved for attention all of my life and NOW I was getting it. I was getting more than I could handle.

I had become bitter about my husband's lack of interest in me and realized that I had developed a new attitude. Actions that showed and attitude of "you don't care so I won't care". I now realized that my feelings were right all along. Feelings that I was second place or even 4th or 5th to him. First place to him was either alcohol or drugs, second place was his desire to be successful and third place was his desire to have free time to play softball, golf or whatever else struck him.

I began a lifestyle that was very opposite to the past eleven years. I desired to be at work, with men who showed me that I was good at something and that I was beautiful and sexy. I enjoyed the officers that I worked with more than being around my husband. When he saw that I was wanting to be gone on Friday nights to work, then he began feeling left out and wanted me at home. But I deserved my time, I felt! After all, where was he all those other weekends and evenings when I sat at home crying because he didn't spend time with me. I felt that this would be good for our marriage, being gone and letting him experience what I had in the past 10 years. Maybe he would learn how to seek me out and appreciate me more!

I had even sunk to a point that I thought that I was falling in love with another man. Yes, one from work. The one that always seemed to understand me so well and told me how beautiful I was all the time. He had even offered to help me to get away from Ray when Ray began being abusive. Yes, abusive! He was drinking on a nightly basis by now and if he didn't have any money buy alcohol or an excuse to be gone so that he could drink, then he indulged in our "Nyquil". When I began noticing that the "Nyquil" bottle was empty, I would ask every member of the family if they had used it. The children all denied using and I believed that they were being truthful because I had always taught them to come to me if they needed ANY medications. When I asked him if he had emptied the bottle, he would always deny it, but I began noticing that the bottles were empty and no one had even been sick to have to use it. I had to start storing it at my neighbors house so that we would have it if we ever needed it. We began to have some extremely heated arguments where the police had to be called to prevent him from becoming more abusive. After a few visits from the police, they became familiar with our situation. They knew that I was an officer and that he was prone to become disorderly if he was intoxicated. His violent behavior had gotten to the point where that I was afraid to even go to sleep. I lived in constant fear!

Because of my feelings of guilt for my recent behaviors, I began to believe that I was deserving of his abuse now, especially when I awoke at three o'clock in the morning with the bright bedroom light in my eyes and there was Ray standing beside me by our bed, holding a gun to his head. He began screaming at me about how I had pushed him to this point since he heard my telephone conversation with the man from work. The conversation he heard was when I told him that I believed that I loved him, and asked him to wait and give me time to find out what I was going to do with my present marriage. Ray went off the deep end when he heard that. I can certainly understand that this would have driven me crazy too, but not enough to kill! I hoped that he was just trying to gain my attention with the gun and not really serious. I began begging and pleading with him to put the gun away and telling him that we could work things out! That was evidently not the right thing to say because he then turned the gun on me and I was now looking down the barrel of my own duty weapon!!! I began crying and screaming for his forgiveness and pleading for my own life and trying to say anything to calm him, but all he could do is to tell me that he couldn't trust me and that I was just a big liar and that he didn't have to put up with someone like me. Then for some reason, he turned the gun back on himself. I tried to get to the telephone to dial 911, but as I neared it, he jerked it away! Then, strangely enough, he calmed down and put the gun away and told me that I wasn't worth it (meaning jail or death). He walked off and I wasn't sure what was going to happen next. During all this scene, I realized that my misdeeds brought this about. He was only gone for a moment and came back with a recording device and showed me what he had been doing.

He had been recording all of my telephone calls for the past few months. That is why he would occasionally wake me at two or three a.m. and begin questioning and quizzing me and beginning big fights about my answers to his questions. I was so very ashamed! He now knew all about my little escapades when I was running around and doing my own pleasure. I was grossly ashamed, even though that while I was doing all this, I felt justified because of his actions! If he was going to care less about me and the family, then I didn't feel that I should try to be a faithful loyal wife anymore. But the big difference between him and me was that my relationship with God wouldn't allow me to continue in this lifestyle.

This big scene occurred about 10 months, after I had begun being untruthful to him about my whereabouts. He now was approaching me with the threat of divorce and that he now had the taped evidence to take to court so that he could prove that I was unfit to have custody of the children. I was now really terrified!!! I never wanted to lose my children and there was absolutely nothing that was worth losing them! I quickly surrendered everything. I first told him that I really didn't love the man, but that I was just looking for a way out to help me to leave. I told him that I would call him immediately and tell him the truth and tell him that we would never speak to each other again. Then I told him that I would give up my Police Career and turn in all of my equipment soon as day broke. When I said that, he looked at me and asked me if I was serious. I told him that I was very serious and that I never wanted our marriage to go bad in the first place. All I ever wanted to be was a wife, with a Christian family to love and take care of. I knew that it would take this, to make him believe that I was serious about making things work, because he kept telling me that my Police Work was OUR problem and that if I quit, then we would be fine. Out of desperation to do whatever it would take to mend things, I quit, that very next morning! I reluctantly quit, but if this would straighten up our marriage and prove my love for him, then I would do it. I had plunged myself back into church work and being a housewife. Our business was still going, but after filing bankruptcy, there wasn't much left. I felt like I had made the ultimate sacrifice, knowing that my job wasn't our problem. His drinking had started back 2 or 3 years prior to that. I knew that THE DRINKING was our problem!

After a few weeks, I knew that I had made the biggest mistake of my life. It seemed that our goals to repair our marriage had become one-sided again. I was trying with 100% of my efforts. He was putting in very little effort. He was drinking and staying out just like before. I became so angry and confused at this point! Nothing had changed but me! Even though I was confused about my marriage, I was no longer confused about my focus toward my original goals, my spiritual walk and raising my children.

A few months later, I had finally reached the point that I knew our marriage was over. I had lost respect for him, totally, by this point. Now, I was losing respect for myself. I was so afraid of him that I didn't proceed with the first divorce papers that I had filed several months prior. He wasn't even aware of them, because I cancelled the process before he was served. I was afraid that I would lose my children because he and his mother had said that they would do whatever it would take, to keep me from having the kids. His mother was capable of doing whatever she said! He knew that the key to keeping me where he wanted me was by threatening to withhold my children from me. He had even threatened to leave the country so that no one would ever find them. I believed him for a long time. This is why I remained in the marriage, enduring abuse and violence.

I finally got the courage to file for a divorce a second time, and this time, he was served with papers. The paper work included a Protective Order so that he could be arrested if he tried to come near me or the children, until our hearing. I hoped and prayed that this would work. I had also obtained a full time job for the Everman Police Department and I was to start just a few days after the papers were served to him. I felt that I had all everything in line and ready to make the escape work and to protect the kids from being used as pawns. We even went to stay in a Women's Shelter to avoid all danger!

We spoke by telephone and this is how I told him that I was leaving with the children. He saw that all of our clothes were gone from the house and he realized that I was serious. He began promising that he would quit drinking and that we would go to counseling. I wanted to believe him, but I knew that he would say anything to get us back. Did he really mean what he had said? He hadn't followed through with any of his past promises. I was determined to stand firm this time.

There was only one problem. My proper reasoning told me that we needed to leave for our safety and our future, but my heart could not let go. We had been together for nearly 14 years! I just couldn't bear to leave him and for the kids to lose their father after he promised me that he would go for counseling AND quit drinking. This is what I really wanted! I wanted to feel secure in our marriage and I knew that if he really would quit drinking and would go to counseling, then our marriage had a chance. He had told me that he didn't want me to take the job at Everman, but I told him that I was going to take the job because I had no guarantee that he would keep his word! He tried very hard to persuade me otherwise, but finally I stood up for what I thought was right. I promised him that I would drop the divorce papers after a few months, but that I was going to keep the job for two years, and that this would help me to feel certain that he was really going to quit drinking and that our marriage would change! He finally agreed to my terms.

He even took me to a wedding shop, as a surprise, and told me that I was to pick out a wedding dress because he wanted us to have the wedding that he had denied me in our beginning. He wanted us to a wedding ceremony on our 13th Anniversary. I wasn't too sure about the wedding ceremony though. I had always wanted something like this before things had gotten so bad, but I was leery of doing this now. I was determined to do whatever it took though and if he wanted to do this, then I would happily comply, even if I did feel foolish making all these plans. I had five and half months to prepare for it, or cancel it, if necessary.

Maybe he was sincere this time. We went to one counseling session together. I went to three or four after that, but he didn't want to go anymore. He insisted that everything was fine now. I prayed that the Lord would take the bitterness that I felt inside, about all the past things that he had done, away from me. I was getting much stronger in my relationship with God and in putting my entire focus on our marriage.

Well, I had planned a beautiful, but simple wedding in our church. I had even written a song to him to reconfirm my love and dedication to him and I sang it to him at the renewal ceremony. We didn't get to have a second honeymoon afterward though, just a one night stay in a simple hotel. He told me that he was really happy about the wedding and that he was sorry that we hadn't started it off right from the beginning.

He had gone for 5 and half months without drinking (that I know of) before this Renewal ceremony, but a few months later, he started drinking socially again. I had warned him that I didn't think that it was a great idea, but he told me that he had things under control. Something was under control!

He was!!! After another few months had passed, he was back to drinking on a regular basis. He was drinking at the softball fields again and at the pool hall by his new job. He had a new Maintenance Manager position for the past several months and a Pool hall had opened at the site where he worked. How convenient. He had always loved pool! In the month of July, the kids and I had only seen Ray a couple of times because he was staying at one place or the other until they closed down and he would come in so late at night (or early in the morning) that the kids didn't even know that he had been there. I was really getting scared. He had even confessed to me that, one night, he met a man at the pool hall who offered to sell him some drugs and guns. Ray said that he had to smoke a joint with this man because this was the only way to find out about all of his other illegal sales that he was doing. Ray's reasoning was that he wanted to turn the information over to the police. That was a clever excuse to go back and participate in the old "Drug of Choice!" When he told me that, I just crumbled inside. He was headed right back down to the bottom. He had begun to lie about his activities to try to cover up.

I knew now, that it was over! I couldn't go back to living this way again, AND I wouldn't let myself be taken down with him. I was still serving the Lord and giving all of my attention to my family. I had kept the job, (thank goodness!) and now I was really going to need it.

I called the attorney back and began the paper work again. My dad had helped me financially, to obtain the legal work, and he warned me that I had better follow through this time because I wouldn't get his help again. He wanted us to either make it, or stop. Dad wasn't one to advise anyone to get a divorce, but he saw that this was hopeless and wanted the kids to feel safe again. My biggest problem that I had with Ray's drinking was that I was living in fear again. I never knew what state of mind he would come home in. The type of abuse he frequently used was mental. He liked to make me think that I was losing my mind or to have me feel helpless. He was beginning to start up some of those habits again.

August 4, 1992, was when the divorce papers and protective orders were served to him and he knew that it was really over this time. He wasn't going to be nice about it though! He put us through hell again. Dad came to stay with us for a while to help out. We had to be careful that Ray wouldn't abduct the kids, in spite of another Protective Order. Ray told me that we were going to have to move from the house, because he was going to sell it. I was willing to do whatever he asked, just so long as we could have a peaceful divorce. I wanted him to sign the papers so I agreed to all of his terms, even a ridiculously low child support amount!

Dad's support during this time was extremely helpful to me and to the children. He seemed to help us feel secure during this transition. He had been up, just the month before, to visit and to get away from Mom. He had told me that she was causing him to feel so stressed out, that he wanted to jump out of his skin. He said that he was wondering if he was going to have a nervous breakdown because she was driving him crazy. He saw how cruel she spoke to and treated the elderly people that she was taking care of in their home. She had told Dad that she wanted to take care of elderly people in their home for some added income. He was against this, because he was retired and was ready to relax and enjoy life together. To retire, meant to her, that she wouldn't be able to do all the things to her house to make it the finest home in the city. They had moved out to Ft. Davis in 1984 to retire there. This was a very small town and she found that it would be much easier to be on the top of the social ladder there because it was a relatively poor town. She wanted THE biggest, best, and the finest home in the entire area! So she knew that she would have to work to get it because Dad wanted a simpler life-style. She was treating the old people like dirt. She yelled and screamed at them as though they were animals. Totally disrespectful of their age and the fact that their families were paying her to CARE for them. Anyway, when I told Dad that the paperwork was in the attorney's hands again, he had agreed to be there to help.

Mom was so angry and jealous that he had come to stay with me for a few weeks, that she stepped in and began causing trouble for us. Dad had become the Justice of the Peace in the County and she called up the Child Protective Services and reported to them that my dad was sexually molesting and assaulting all three of my children while he was with us! Can you believe that!?! How could anyone accuse her husband of something like that? She knew that he was only going to help out his daughter and grandchildren! CPS began an immediate investigation on Dad and me and the CPS workers had to go to my children's schools to investigate the allegations. Mom got help from Ray's Mother to do all of this! Ray's mother tried to turn the kids away from their Grandpa, but her scheme failed miserably!!! The only thing that their efforts caused was a termination of the relationship that they had with me and the children! PERMANENTLY!!!

Mom also filed for a divorce stating that Dad had abandoned her and that she was afraid that he would come back to harm her. I knew my Dad very well. Some of the things that she had done to him and us, in the past, would have called for any normal man to have lost control and strike her, but he NEVER did that. He was the most self-controlled man I had ever known!!! She was accusing him of something that was totally out of his character and against his nature!

I was furious! Ray's mother was going to use something like this to try to take the children away from me. How could either of these Grandmothers ever put their grandchildren through something like this? I detested the fact that Mom's jealousy lead her to do something that would try to hurt my children. She had done plenty of things in the past to hurt me, things for which I had forgiven her, but she was NOT going to ever hurt my children! I called her and told her that she had just paid for a permanent denial of her rights to ever be considered my mom again or my children's grandmother. I told her that I could never have anything to do with her again. For my children's protection, I would sever my ties forever. From that point, she was history!

Dad was actually relieved, somewhat, with her filing for divorce. He didn't think that he could witness any more of her cruelty and rudeness to others or himself. He didn't want to face life alone though. He was nearing 70 years old. He didn't want to grow old lonely, but he didn't want to grow old feeling miserable and tied up in knots either!

Dad stayed long enough to help me and the children to move into a mobile home near my job. This meant taking the children out of their school and away from their friends. I hated it that Ray wouldn't let us stay there.

In October, I almost lost my rational thinking! On our anniversary, I became very depressed. I had been regretting our divorce. Divorce was a philosophy that went against the Biblical principals that I believed in. The children were torn up, even though they tried not to show it. I called to talk to him, for the first time since we had separated, and I asked him if there was anyway we could reach a reconciliation. I couldn't believe that those words came out of my mouth. But at the same time, I couldn't stop the rush of emotions going through my heart and mind that day.

We agreed to go out to dinner and we planned to sit and talk about the possibility. The kids were excited too. We went out to eat dinner together and then went to his apartment afterwards to talk. The kids left us alone and we looked at each other and without saying a word, we both began to cry. We just couldn't believe that after 14 years of being married, we had to have this kind of ending. Both of said that we didn't want to divorce, so we asked each other if we could start again. We agreed that the next morning, we would make plans to come back together. We even made the announcement to the kids, that we were getting back together. Ray dropped us off at the mobile home around 11:00 pm that night because he said that he needed to sleep since he hadn't been sleeping for a few days. He told me that he had nearly lost his job also, because he just couldn't go to sleep and when he finally would, he wouldn't be able to wake up to hear his alarm. I knew that he needed his wife again to help him with that.

The next morning, Ray came to pick up the kids to stay with him for the day, until I got off from work. When he arrived, he smelled like a brewery!!! I couldn't believe it!!! It was obvious that he had been drinking very heavily after he dropped us off last night, because the alcohol smell was coming from his stomach! How could he? Here we were, making happy plans of reuniting and he goes off to drink! He had told me that he was just nervous about everything, but that he would be fine.

Well I wasn't fine! An eerie feeling came over me that scared the daylights out of me. I felt that I had been totally deceived the night before by all his talk about getting back together and all. It was as though someone had just lifted off the blinders and I was staring reality right in the face! HE WAS NEVER GOING TO QUIT DRINKING!!! NOT EVEN TO SAVE HIS MARRIAGE!

That evening, I told him that I was sorry, but that the reconciliation was off. I told him that his drinking that night had given me the sign that I had been praying for. I had asked the Lord to show me that I was doing the right thing but instead he showed me the opposite and I took it as a firm warning!

Ray was so angry. He told me that I got his hopes up for nothing and that he hated my guts. He told me to bring him those divorce papers immediately so that he could sign them because he wouldn't take me back now, even if I begged.

Well, I didn't hesitate. He signed them all and I went straight to the courts with them for a final hearing.

On November 11, 1992, our marriage was legally ended. He didn't show up for court, which was good for me. I don't believe that I would have had the emotional strength to endure it, had Ray been there. I walked out of the courtroom with such a sense of relief but also a sense of remorse. I knew that I had done the right thing, but it was so sad to know that 14 years of my life was closed, except for the children. They were the bright spots of those 14 years! They were worth it all, and now I had responsibility to see to it that the divorce was going to be an improvement for all of us. I knew that the court had given us joint custody and awarded me a menial support for them, but I didn't feel that he would ever keep his end of the bargain.

I was right again! He never came to see the kids anymore, NOT EVEN for Christmas! His support payments stopped shortly after that.

I wasn't able to keep up with my commitment to the Lord about being 100% faithful. After Ray and I separated, I found out that I wasn't cut out to be single. Dating again, was no different than when I was 17 and 18. Men only wanted one thing from women and I had a difficult time telling them no! I hated the reality of it. I had come to the point where I was on my knees crying and begging God to forgive me and change my circumstances because I was too weak to try any longer. I actually felt like taking my own life again, but I had three beautiful children that depended on me for their own lives. They were all that kept me from closing the book that evening. I told God that I couldn't do the "single thing" and remain a righteous Christian woman. I was powerless! I knew that I had to call on the power of God to take control and I did. I screamed to God for mercy to end this before I destroyed myself. I had already learned that being a wife and mother was all that made me feel complete. I detested waiting for some date to call and then to later find out if I met his approval. If I didn't meet all of his expectations, then I would be discarded like a piece of trash. My need for affection and love was very strong and no matter how real God was to me, I couldn't feel Him. I told God that He already knew that I was impatient and stupid, but that I had to be honest with him. I told Him that I really needed a father for these children. Randall, Joel and Rachel were at the age that they needed a stable father. I also told Him that I needed a husband and I knew that it was too soon to ask, but I needed Him to take control of me until He gave me one. I asked God to bring a man into the kids life, that would fill the void of their own dad being gone, until He found them a stepfather. I recognized my weaknesses and helplessness. Without God's control, I would surely destroy myself AND all the Spiritual values and lessons that I had taught my children.

Only three weeks later, I met the man! The man that God would bring as a blessing to us to be my husband and my children's father. It was truly love at first sight for me. He was a Christian man WITH values. He never tried to use me or treat me without the utmost respect. What captured my heart from the beginning, was when we met, he asked me if I had any kids. Thinking that would run as fast as he could when he heard my answer, I reluctantly said, "Yes." I was floored by his response! He said in a very excited voice, "You do! How many?" I just new that this answer had to be the one to set him running! I looked up and said, "Three!" He said, "That's great! How old are they?" "Oh why did he have to ask that," I thought, "Surely he won't be excited about three preteens." But instead, his response was of delight. He told me that he wanted to meet them and how he loved kids. He went on and on about how lucky I was to have children and how special it was to be a mother and on and on! I had never met a man like this! I was awestruck!

He was serious about meeting the kids. Two days later, he asked if we could go out WITH the kids. They were a little apprehensive about meeting another one of my dates. They hadn't liked a single one of the others. In fact, they would do everything possible to keep me away from them.

This was different though! They were instantly taken by him! They had so much fun that they were asking him, when would be the next time that they would see him. He was willing to come by and see them the next day. They fell in love with him immediately.

I felt like I was being visited by a Prince! We saw each other every single day. We enjoyed every moment together and dreaded every moment apart! We had a very close bond. Each of us had a desire to feel loved and to give love.

Within a few months, we were married!

It was as though God had told me to open my hands and close my eyes and that I would be given the biggest blessing that I could ever begin to behold. The treasured blessing at the end of a rainbow, just handed to Me! The Lord had heard my prayer and given me an immediate answer! I never expected Him to respond immediately. After all, I had waited for 14 years for the last husband to be changed by Him.

Our lives were changed forever! Changed from lives of uncertainty, to lives filled with love and happiness!

There had been a major hurdle to conquer though. He was an Adventist! I wasn't anymore. I had decided to never be an Adventist again, after living that life with Bee. She had taught me that an Adventist Christian was a miserable existence. Every Friday night was hell! Living up to her strict guide-lines of what a Christian teen should wear, how they should look and the things they shouldn't do. Since then, I have learned more about Christ and I learned that he is not a God of bondage.

My new husband understood my perspective of the Adventist lifestyle when he heard me tell of some of the horrors of living with Bee! He told me that in So. Africa, where he was born and raised, the Adventist people served God out of love and knew of the same relationship that I had learned of at the Living Word Center.

We came to an agreement. I would go to church with him on Saturdays and he would go to church with me on Sundays. It wouldn't hurt us to do this. So that was how we managed for over a year.

Then the Lord had spoken to me about serving in the Adventist Church. I had been a Youth leader in the Living Word Center for 9 years and helped serve in many other areas faithfully, as well. I also loved singing in the church. I knew that the Lord had given me a talent of teaching and dealing with young people, especially troubled teens. My police career had even turned in that direction as I had been a impact on many teens by counseling them and teaching them D.A.R.E. (Drug Abuse Resistance Education). I kept arguing with God that I couldn't serve in the church unless I was a member. The Lord continued to call and finally I decided to change my membership to the Adventist church. I didn't quite agree with everything, but I had found a different church than what I had experienced years ago. I found a message of

God's love and grace. I was feeling so alive again by the words that I heard spoken in the Pastor's messages. Eventually, I knew that God had called me back, not only to serve, but to experience the true message! God does love us and wants each of us to serve Him and to spread His message of love to everyone else, to prepare them for His soon return!

We now have two children together also. This gives me five children in all! I am so very blessed. All five of the children live with us. Ben has been a wonderful father to them and a life saver for the teens. Randall and Joel had always wanted a Dad to do things with them. They definitely found that in Ben. He was firm but he loved them as his very own flesh and blood. He treats them as HIS children and spoils them at times as though he has been given a terrific honor to be allowed a part in their lives. His firmness has helped them to learn respect and proper direction. The two younger children's names are Benjamin, now 4 years old, and Ashley Ranae, who is two and half years old. Yes, I am finished having children! Five children are is far more than I had ever dreamed of having. My limit was two, or so I thought. Five is a handful, but the love from each of them is so very rewarding!

I now know what love and affection are. I receive plenty of it from my husband and five children. I also receive love from so many friends in our church families and from Ben's parents. Oh how sweet it is to live in the shadows of His blessings! Oh what joy to know what real love is, how to receive and how to give it.

Chapter 12: The Purpose

Because of my past, I was nearly handicapped. Not physically but emotionally! I had very little understanding of what true love was and the understanding that I did possess, was warped! I couldn't stand to be held in anyone's arms for very long, not even by my husband. When I was a teen, church members would try to hug me and I would feel uncomfortable. I certainly didn't know how to caress my husband or even my own baby. That may sound odd considering that I sought the love of a boyfriend to fill the void in my life, but it was more of a social and emotional love rather than physical. I was very shy of physical touch. That was one of the reasons that my relationship with Kurt was so very special. I was able to be touched and hugged by him and I never felt uncomfortable. He had no demands and I felt at ease with him. You would think that it would be so simple to express love to an infant then. But infants are demanding! I found that out on Randall's first night at home. I felt frustrated because I didn't know what to do to make him happy and to top it off, when I was ready to put him down, he wasn't!

I had also "learned" to lie about anything that might bring trouble my way. You see, it didn't matter if I told the truth or not, the consequences would always be the same. If I told the truth, there were no rewards or slack in the amount of discipline I would have to endure, so, it was better to lie and hope that I wouldn't get caught! To Mother, accidental or intentional, it was all the same. All she cared was that I was the one to blame for her being inconvenienced!

I had also "learned" to never look anyone in the eye. UNLESS, I was lying that is! I got very good at looking a parent directly in the eye and then lie through my teeth. I was never asked to look into her eyes for anything else and I was shamed so badly, that I had a habit of looking downward when I spoke. As a teen, I learned to look in a person's direction, but not directly into their eyes. My habit was so bad, that I had failed to realize what beautiful eyes Ray had until someone mentioned them. I knew that they were blue, but I had never known the content of his eye. If anyone asked to see my eyes, such as for a picture, I would shy away.

I "learned" to disregard certain types of yelling or screaming. There were only certain pitches that really got my attention. The others were tuned out, so that I could bear the noise.

I "learned" that I was never good enough to even attempt to try my best because my best was never satisfactory. Besides, if I did well for a while, it was a wasted attempt because Mom would always throw up my entire past to prove that I wasn't worth trusting. I had no hope in becoming trustworthy. It was a pointless cause.

I "learned" to work for favors. If I wanted to get any favors from Mother or Bee, I would have to do something really big to earn it. I didn't mind doing my share of the workload, but it was much easier to sneak off, than to face the extra work to earn the privilege. I believe that this method is an appropriate means for certain privileges, but there always needs to be some free-bees. A "just because I love you" sort of thing!

I "learned" to be impatient with others, especially my own children. I was never tolerant of slow-minded thinkers or slow moving doers. This was a great source of irritation to me. "Do it and do it now!" "AND DO IT RIGHT THE FIRST TIME!" These became my mottos, forgetting, that simple instructions are sometimes necessary for inexperienced workers. It is so simple to bark out an order and expect it to be done though. If you are dissatisfied with the work, just scream and yell for them to redo it and they'll eventually get it right!

I "learned" to scream whenever I was frustrated. This way, people would know my dilemma and rush to assist. I had forgotten that this forces people away instead of drawing them in to assist.

I had "learned" that God was very punitive. I thought that He had a big tally sheet where he would make a mark for my bad deeds and then erase one for the seldom good deeds. This view of God caused me a lot of frustration. I read my Bible regularly, but not for understanding. I only read to be accepted by Him.

I "learned" that proving your best to others, is far more important than pleasing your family. Even at my families' expense. They will just have to understand! My reputation to others is important!

I "learned" the edge of competitiveness! To be the best! The only way you gain attention or approval is by outdoing everyone else. Second place never gets attention!

I "learned" that I could gain attention by telling my sad story of being mistreated and unloved and even being molested! I could literally captivate people with the hair raising stories. I didn't even have to embellish, just tell it straight out! People would always tell me how sorry they were for me! If they quit giving me attention, then I would just have to do something else to make them feel sorry for me again!

I "learned" that my past was also a very good excuse for me to quit trying when the "going got tough". If I did succeed at something, I had learned not to shout in triumph because misery followed right behind.

I "learned" to be quite shallow about other's feelings because I only saw my own problems most of the time. I couldn't be a close friend because I was always thinking of myself and my needs since they seemed so overwhelming! By the time that I had finished talking about all my problems, there wasn't much time left for theirs, if they felt like telling me, after all that I had unloaded on them. I wasn't there to listen to them and their needs, as a good friend should. I was always the one talking instead of listening.

I never "learned" how to take a compliment. If I was ever complimented, there was usually some underlying method or joke to it. I learned to have a quick "comeback" ready for them if they had their punch line loaded.

I "learned" to be very good at sarcasm. I had heard a lot in my youth.

I had learned the life of a Chameleon, the lizard who blends in with his surroundings. I learned that in order to fit in and be accepted, I could just change my mannerisms and personality and WAH LAH! An instant piece to any puzzle! My father-in-law first noticed this trait and made mention of it to me. I was very embarrassed that it was so obvious. When I would be around Ray's family, I would talk crudely and act more masculine, so that his step mom would accept me. She didn't like me, at first, because I was from a different economic class and she commented that I was a snob. I had never been called that before. She just didn't feel comfortable with someone out of her economic class but that didn't mean I was a snob. I tried to fit in so I changed to be more rough, like she was. I would act more "polished" when I was around other people of a higher status. I would act more saintly around those that needed to see that side of me. I had so many sides that I didn't know who I was.

Yet, with all that I had learned, I knew that I was empty. I knew that there had to be more to life than misery and futility.

I searched high and low for my much needed answers to one simple question. Why was God allowing me to suffer like this? From this question came a few others, such as, when would it end? Had I done something to deserve this lot in life?, What was the point in continuing on in life?

Everyone that I asked said basically the same thing. Either, "I don't know why" or "God doesn't want anyone to suffer, but since sin entered the world, we all have our share in the suffering". They would always add that God is always there to give us strength and that He would never put more on us than we can bear. It wasn't the answer that I was looking for. I needed deeper answers. Why was all this happening to me?!? When would it all end?!? Doesn't He think that I had endured my share yet?

Unfortunately, even those who were trained in the Ministry weren't able to give me the answer.

The purpose of my tragedies was to seek the answer!

I have learned the answer now. It's not a simple answer, but it is THE answer. I am certainly not pompous enough to tell you that I have all the answers though. God doesn't always have each person walk the same road to get to the same ending. Others may go through similar tragedies or trials but be led by the Spirit to learn different lessons. However, ultimately we all must learn the same answer. I wouldn't dare give you the answer yet. That might cause you to put the book down with only a formula that you may think will apply for every given situation.

Chapter13: The Answer

I had been headed the right way on several occasions but always met with the Chief Deceiver along the way. He turned me onto the wrong path each time that I got near the right answer.

It WAS in the Word of God. Not simply reading the Bible though.

It WAS in church attendance also, but not solely.

It WAS in helping others, but not for their approval.

It WAS in proving your best to others but realizing that the PROOF is NOT in you.

It WAS in seeking counsel from Christian workers, but not expecting them to have every answer. Their prayers for support, wisdom and direction, that they prayed for God to give me, were very beneficial.

It was none of these items singly and not even cumulatively. There was more!

It was a *relationship* with my Creator! You can't read His Book for entertainment or just to say that you've done so. Without the Spirit of God, the words are dead. My relationship with Him would develop by picking up His letters (the Bible) to His people and truly *desiring* to know Him, by reading His inspired words. Realizing that He gave us the Word so that we could know the right steps to take. If we take the steps that go along with His will for us, then we will have real joy. God's Word is not a book of Don'ts but a book of Do's. I had always thought that if we did what the Word said, then we would stay out of trouble from Him, but my thinking was totally wrong. He desires for us to live a happy, fulfilled life and that is, in spite of our trials. When we are in the Will of God, we have peace. It's only when we are seeking the will of ourselves, that we feel the stress, turmoil and emptiness that serving self has to offer.

You must literally desire (with all your heart, not just a piece of it) to be transformed by Him into what He has planned for you. My relationship would develop by prayer (not just when I was in a jam), to talk to God about anything and everything. Literally speaking - the good, the bad and the ugly!

At times I would feel that there wasn't much use in praying since God knew everything anyway. I would only ask Him for the things that I needed, never sharing in special times. But I learned that God would actually take time out for me, to speak to me. Of course it wasn't audibly, but I knew that it was God because He was teaching me and showing me His principles and His wisdom through my surroundings and my inner being! I learned that the few moments that I spent with Him were literally the power surge of the day. I felt the fulfillment in my life that I had been searching for. I felt His love and His care, but more importantly, I received wisdom and answers. If He didn't give me an answer right then, when I asked, he would give me the power and strength that I needed to make it through another day. Only one day though, because if He were to give me more than was sufficient for one day, I would get too busy to come again the next day. He desires our attention as much as we desire to receive His attention. He waits patiently though, while our immaturity causes us to act like idiots sometimes. We finally get desperate enough to remember to go back to our knees in prayer!

It was in my relationship to other brothers and sisters in Christ that would actually cause my relationship with Him to be fulfilled. The relationship with other Christian friends was to be one on a two-way street. Service to each other! I find that Christian relationships are so much more rewarding and meaningful than with those in the world. The world only understands ONE philosophy and that is SELF. When you pour your heart out to a person who is not in tune with the Lord, their advice will always be centered around SELF.

It was also in my service to fellow brothers and sisters. However, what may outwardly appear to be helping someone else, may be filled with many underlying motives. If we benefit from our works, then it is very possible that our motives are not pure, such as, always being the volunteer to assist in the church so that you may one day be asked to become a deacon or deaconess. You have gained in status before the brethren. The Bible warns us that we should always do our service in secret (Matthew 6:4), not boasting of ourselves. If we do this, we have traded in our Heavenly rewards that are eternal for the temporary satisfaction of the praise of men (Matthew 6:1). Motives of the heart are the whole key to a life filled with joy. If our motives are pure, to be what we were designed to be by our Creator, then we will have joy and peace. I didn't say that we would be trouble free. Joy and peace can be present in the midst of the most terrific storm! This is where many Christian people deceive themselves. I know of so many that serve God by living a good life, but it isn't to be right with God, it is motivated by their desire to seek approval from either their fellow church or family members or to avoid the gates of hell. That isn't what God wants for us. That is a dull and even exasperating lifestyle! We will never meet His approval, no matter how hard we try. Our efforts are as filthy rags in God's eyes if we fail to have HIM work those efforts through us! (Isaiah 64:6) We just don't have the capacity within us to do ANY good without His Spirit operating through us. It may appear to human minds that our deeds were good, but God knows the motives of our heart. So often, we seek rewards of praise for our goodness, when in all actuality, we can never accept praise if we realize that the ONLY goodness in us comes from Him and He deserves the praise, NOT US! Therefore, our service to each other is merely allowing God to work in us to benefit our brothers and sisters. That is His direct way to show us love. He uses our hands to serve them, and our minds and mouth to speak words of encouragement to them, and our arms to give them the physical hug they may need from Him. When you see your friends in this light, it totally changes your perspective of a Friendship! It totally changes our perspective!

It was also in my service to mankind that I found my own problems diminished. After seeing the suffering of others, my own suffering seemed less important. *I was set free of being absorbed in my own troubles as I reached out and began helping others with their troubles. Self pity is an ever consuming fire that will destroy every ounce of joy that God intends for us to have.* I have been able to counsel with others who are in extreme circumstances and are crippled by their own self pity. In my counsel to them, I remind them that God carries our load and frees us to be able to help others. Self pity must be rebuked! It is not a part of God's plan for successful, joyous living! If you are indulging in self pity, I encourage you ask for forgiveness and give God the load of hurt and pain, then get involved in helping others so that you will not be tempted to sit idly and begin dwelling on your circumstances again.

My relationship with my Creator would cause me to desire to give my very best in everything that I set my hands and mind to do, because of my witness to others. Because of my relationship with Him, this would give me the desire to please Him and others because His Spirit gives us all the equipment needed to fulfill the course that He has set before us, including the desire to do it! Without Him, I don't even have the desire to give anything, much less, my very best. It is merely a reality that I am yielding my body to allow Him to do His work through me. Therefore, ALL the credit goes to Him.

It is also in accepting the facts. The world is in it's imperfect state. The state of sin. It only has temporary satisfactions to offer but not real fulfillment. We will suffer in this world because of the fallen state. Why would we ever appreciate Heaven, if we were perfectly comfortable on earth? Even in it's fallen state, this earth hasn't been stripped of all it's beauty , and this is where so many are also deceived. Some are trying to devour the beauty and enjoyment of this world and are robbing themselves of the better world to come.

Understanding God's real plan is also a big key. Is it God's will that no one should suffer? I don't think so! Every time I read the Bible, I see suffering of one kind or another. Especially Christ's life! We must also realize that if we partake in His sufferings, then this is a sign to us that we are His. It is a promise to us that if we suffer with Him then we will be glorified with Him and reign with Him forever! (Romans 8:16-18, 2 Timothy 2:12) John 16:33 tells us that in this world we will have tribulation. It never tells us (in context of Scripture) that He meant for us to live a carefree life of ease on this earth. He never told us that we are all to be healthy, wealthy, and wise, either. Those are Satan's tools to lead people astray. Satan will easily send riches and ease to anyone, in order to deceive them. Satan doesn't care if you are happy during this life because he sees the big picture, eternity! You see, Satan's message points to temporary happiness for yourself. The meaning of happiness is derived from the word "happening" which means that an event has occurred to make you happy. When the event is gone though, the happiness goes with it. Joy, on the other hand is not from a happening, but a "state of being", that will last as long as you are connected to the Source. The Source is Christ. It would be nice that all could be healed, but Christ merely promised us that we would have His strength to endure. Sometimes our afflictions lead us to a closer relationship with Christ because we then learn how dependent we really must be upon Him. Without needing Him, we would all go astray. If we had all of our needs met, we would never call out to him. Our pain and sufferings are actually the "blessing in disguise". Our sufferings lead us to Him and our prosperity usually lead us to ourselves.

Just think of this! If you knew a Christian friend, that never had a problem or care about life and he told you that he believed in Jesus, but had no proof of needing to rely on Christ, how real would his testimony be? If you knew another Christian friend, who seemed to have several tragedies occur and he kept his faith in Christ, through thick and thin, wouldn't that make a stronger statement to you about his faith? Or, turning the table, you found a person who was not a believer, and everything in his life seemed perfect. Would he be interested in a Savior? He wouldn't even believe that he had a need for one because his life is just fine like it is. I don't want anybody to think that I look forward to more suffering or that a person must be closer to the Lord if they suffer more. I just believe that suffering has its purpose.

Gold is purified by fire! The hotter the fire gets, the more trash that is burned out, thus making the gold more pure. What is faith? We will never know what faith is without the test of sufferings and pain. Without the test, our faith is WORTHLESS! You can talk it all you want, but until you walk it and it passes God's test, it doesn't exist! "He does not cast worthless stones into His furnace. It is valuable ore that He refines. The blacksmith puts the iron and steel into the fire that he may know what manner of metal they are. The Lord allows His chosen ones to be placed in the funace of affliction to probe what temper they are of and whether they can be fashioned for His work." (E.G. White, *Ministry of Healing*, p. 471

I later learned that God was perfecting me for His work! I never even suspected that he was training me for this work. Pain is much easier to bear, if there is a purpose. God doesn't always let us in on His plans though. If He did, then it wouldn't require faith. Faith is something that is given as a gift from God and through experiences, God reveals how perfectly He can be trusted. Experience (along with God's Word) is what gives us the ability to step in and help others who are in a similar circumstance.

How could I help any teenager, who wants to run away from home, if I couldn't understand those feelings of desperation that he feels? When he feels that there is no use in trying any longer. When he says that he has tried to get along, but nothing works. I can understand, but also be blatantly honest with him to have him search his heart. He needs to find out if he has merely been trying to satisfy his own self, or is he forgetting to allow God to work through him. I can also point out to him that God is his strength and that Christ never expected him to stand through this alone, God just wants him to let His power take over and do the work through him.

How could I help a new mother, who is afraid that she may abuse her child, if

I didn't understand the overwhelming matters of motherhood. Especially if that mother was an abused child also. Could I give her hope? Well, not I, but I could tell her that Christ can because He did for me! I can prove to her that He will also do the same for her. He will teach her how to love that child and to put herself and her own feelings aside so that she can give of herself to that child, without feeling robbed. She can find such joy in taking care of her baby, even when that baby is exhausting her. Christ's strength begins when hers ends!

Could I tell another teenage girl that she isn't a worthless piece of trash to be discarded because she fell into a boy's arms seeking love and finding out that she was used instead? Is there hope for her? Certainly! Christ loves her so much that He will transform her into person who is esteemed highly by Him because He is worthy! He did for me! I certainly didn't deserve it! I can show her how to find true love. All of her life, she had been deceived to believe that her value was based on how much the boys or men wanted her. Christ teaches girls that they are valuable because He created them and He doesn't create trash! They can actually feel fulfillment in life without ever knowing a relationship with a boy or man.

Could I tell a little girl, who had been abused in the most devastating way, that life can be lived to it's fullest with so much joy. The joy would be so full that she would feel that she couldn't withstand one more blessing! Absolutely! The grossest of sin is one when a person would rob a child of his innocence and even make him feel trapped to keep it a secret for life, to fulfill the perpetrator's own sick lust of the flesh. I can tell them that they aren't spoiled goods, marked for life, because of this tragedy. I can tell them that they don't have to be a victim forever. All circumstances work for the good of them that love Him. Even this one can! I have now found that this only made me more equipped to minister to His people. I actually became a more perfect vessel for Christ's use instead of a cracked pot!

Could I tell young people that running away and getting married is not the answer, no matter if they are living a life of hell at home? Or even running away, to make it on their own, believing that they have the ability to run their own lives better, without any help? Without hesitation! I learned that desperate moves are only temporary Band-Aids for a gushing artery! I can actually direct their eyes to see what they are really seeking. The Holy Spirit can use me to remove the deceptions of Satan from their view and show them the end results. The Holy Spirit can reveal Christ's love and wisdom for their situation.

Could I tell a child, that is defenseless against an adult perpetrator who is verbally or physically abusing him, that life is worth living? Yes I can! I can even give them some wonderful advise about how to take care of their circumstances, and how to obtain the assistance that is out there. I can tell them that their parents need help and may not know how to cope with life's stresses, but God can teach them coping skills. God can even use that child to be instrumental in leading that parent to Him. I am not condoning that the child continue to live in abuse though. God has many ways that He can work to reach the parents. The child needs hope and needs to understand what is happening. The hope is in His Word, but it needs to be explained on a level that the child can understand.

Could I tell anyone, who is considering the use of alcohol, tobacco or drugs to ease their pain or to give them a temporary escape, that it is a TRAP and there is no RELIEF in it? I can't only tell them, but I can show them. Satan has so many vices, out in the world, to cover up pain. But a "cover up" is only temporary and usually doesn't last for more than a few moments. The Holy Spirit uses me to teach others that the reality of using these things, is that it only makes the problem bigger. They added a new problem to their list of already overwhelming problems. If they had trouble dealing with the problems they had, then they certainly cannot cope with an additional problem. Besides, adding the chemicals into your body causes higher stress, mentally and physically. You may have a temporary numbing effect, but it is so much shorter than the long term withdrawal that drives them to desire to be numb again, because the pain of reality is now seeming larger. Chemicals have a way of warping our senses and therefore our logic is very out of proportion. They can learn how to ease the pain by giving it ALL to God. He is more than willing to carry it for them.

Can I tell a couple that marriage is really worth the efforts? Even though I had one to fail, it was worth every bit of the effort. I learned how to focus my dependence on Christ and how to serve Him by serving my husband and then learning to expect nothing in return. I learned the meaning of true giving. I learned how to hang on to Christ in the midst of the most hellacious storm! His rewards for hanging on are far better than the world's advise to divorce. Divorce doesn't change much! You will find that your next marriage will have the same problems in it. If you don't ever learn how to work through the problems, then they will continue to reappear. Do you really think that God is going to teach us faith by plucking us out of the situation when we think that we're through or that we have had enough? Is that how you raise your child, to quit when he thinks that he can't try again? How successful would he turn out to be if you pulled him from every difficulty in life? If you enter a marriage with divorce as an option, then you will always choose it! You have to enter a marriage with only one option. "Till death do we part!" We say it in our vows to each other, but we don't mean it if we see divorce as an alternative to a poor decision.

Triumph, is knowing that God created me with a plan and purpose in mind. He has a path for me to take and as long as I am walking on that path, I have peace and joy, but the moment that I step one foot off that path, confusion and heartache begin. Learning that a human is only capable of doing evil, without the Spirit of God, is the beginning of our greatness. Our greatness occurs only if it is His greatness working through us. Because of His greatness, we are capable of anything. We are more than conquerors because "Greater is He that is within me, than he that is in the world. 1 John 4:4

My tragedy was not because of my sufferings, but it was in my own efforts to handle the problems. My triumph is not in my own achievements, but in His!

"And we know that all things work together for good to them that love God, to them who are the called according to His purpose." Romans 8:28 KJV

It is comforting to fully understand this verse and to know that it applies to you!

There is a song that I sing when I give my testimony called - "Through it all".

Since I cannot sing it for you in a book, then I'll write the words for you to read:

> I've had many tears and sorrows,
> I've had questions for tomorrow,
> There have been times I didn't know right from wrong.

But in every situation,
God gives me blessed consolation,
That my trials come only to make me strong.

I've been alot of places
And I've seen millions of faces,
But there were times when I felt so all alone.
But in my lonely hour,
Yes, those precious lonely hours,
Jesus lets me know that I am his own.
That's the reason I say that
Through it all.
Through it all.
I've learned to trust in Jesus!
I've learned to trust in God!
Through it all.
Through it all.
I've learned to depend upon His word.
I've learned to depend upon His word.

So I thank God for my mountains,
And I thank Him for the valleys,
And I thank him for the storms that He's brought me through.
Oh, if I never had a problem,
I wouldn't know that Jesus could solve them,
And I wouldn't know what faith in His Word is.
And that's the reason I say that
Through it all,
Through it all,
I've learned to trust in Jesus,
and I've learned to trust in God!
Through it all,
Through it all,

> I've learned to depend upon His Word.
>
> I've learned to depend upon His Word.
>
> I've learned to depend, upon His Word!!!

I can truly say that I thank God for every pain that I suffered and for every trial that I endured, because my eternal life is far more important. My joy is full now, but it is by serving Him and in serving Him, I serve others.

I am a Youth Sabbath School teacher and assist in Pathfinders presently. I had also been a youth leader at the Living Word Center for many years. As a Police Officer, I am privileged to step into the classrooms and teach children how to make their lives better. I can give them decision making skills, coping skills, stress relief tips, a sense of hope in their future, a sense of proper self-esteem, and tools make their lives seem worthwhile. I can give them a sense of pride by letting them know that they can achieve dreams and goals far beyond what they ever dreamed of. I am basically a Role-Model to them to show them that just because tragedy and suffering lands in your path doesn't mean life is hopeless and that they should just give up. I am a walking Miracle and anyone who knows me, knows where the credit goes. I hope to inspire others to soar with eagles, because they see me soaring! I have been a guest speaker on many occasions and attempt to use every opportunity to glorify God.

If by chance, I have failed in some way to have you understand that I give all credit to my Father in Heaven, then please forgive me. I want no credit for my successes! I only want to continue to walk on the path that He has set before me so that He may be glorified!

Note: All persons who were in some part responsible for the tragedies incurred have been forgiven by Catherine, however, never forgotten! Some of the names have been changed in order to protect the identity of those who may face embarassment. There is no malice or bitterness in my heart toward anyone that was mentioned in this story.

Dedication:

This book is first dedicated to my Heavenly Father and His Son who has inspired me to write about the Good News of hope! I have truly learned that without Him, I am nothing!

I would not have survived my childhood without the love of my Dad who loved me as though I was his very own flesh and blood! My Dad was the only link that I had with some reality of what true love is. My Dad is the epitome of Love! The man that I will always honor and respect for showing what a real man is!

Next, I would like to dedicate this to my three wonderful teenagers, Randall, Joel and Rachel. Without their patience with me, I would have given up as a mother. They taught me how to feel loved. I thank them for always being so willing to forgive me for all my stupid mistakes. They are a source of inspiration to me every day. I am really proud of them and I only hope that I can live up to being the Mother that they deserve! I don't feel worthy to have been given the opportunity to rear them because they really are GOOD kids! I know that I have been blessed.

Then, to my Wonderful Husband Ben! Oh what it means to be a wife now! A joy that is present through the good times and the bad. Ben let me feel love without demands! He has given my children a direction and a new purpose in life.

My two little babies. Although they really aren't babies now, they are actually toddlers. It just feels so good to rear them in a new light. I have a lot of help from my husband in raising them and I have learned to accept them without being too demanding. It's nice to just be able to love them and spend time with them. Since, I never dreamed of having five children, they must be special to make me truly happy about being a mother of five. I love it!

I must dedicate a portion of this to my closest friends that were there for me when I was going through all this. I know that I talked their ears off and they probably got sick of hearing my problems, but without them, I would have had no one to turn to. My thanks to you, Melissa Wiley, Schantile Grober - McCray, and Cathy Guzman - Reichert and Sue Liles

DeFrancisco. My wonderful Christian neighbors, the Manuels, helped me in the midst of the storm!

I must also dedicate this to the loving Pastoral family - The McGehees, of the Living Word Center, who taught me the depth of Christ's love and mercy and how to really understand God's Word for my life. Their prayers and counseling was always there for me, no matter how busy they were.

My church family can't be left out because they taught me that I had a family right there and that I could live without my physical family being present. I was always accepted and loved.

I must also thank my ex-Father-in-law, Jesse, for being used by God to interrupt me and my own direction and show me that there was a better direction that lead to peace and joy.

I would also like to thank Pastor Everett for showing me that the Adventist church had a message of Love and Mercy that I wasn't aware of before. I praise God for his messages that drove me to hunger for more. He showed me that I had severely misjudged the church and their people because of one bad witness.

I would also like to thank my new Adventist church family for welcoming me back with open arms and allowing me to blossom into my Ministry!

Finally, I would likeMrs. Jodi Robinson for her expertice in the English language. She was so kind to proofread the text of this book for publication. She has known me for many years, but recently she has become a very dear and trusted friend and spiritual mentor. She is truly one that I can turn to for prayer and encouragement.

I am loved so very much!

If you interested in obtaining a copy of this book or obtaining a free copy of the TMC catalog contact

Texas Media Center
1-800-795-7171
www.texasmediacenter.com